# THE COLLECTED WORKS
# OF HERMAN DOOYEWEERD

*Series B, Volume 1*

GENERAL EDITOR:   D.F.M. Strauss

# Christian Philosophy

# and the Meaning of History

Herman Dooyeweerd

The Edwin Mellen Press
Lewiston/Queenston/Lampeter

## Library of Congress Cataloging-in-Publication Data

Dooyeweerd, H. (Herman), 1894-1977.
  [Selections. English. 1997]
  Christian philosophy and the meaning of history / Herman
Dooyeweerd.
    p. cm
  Includes bibliographical references and index.
  ISBN 0-7734-8732-8 (hard)
  1. Philosophy. 2. Christianity--Philosophy. 3. Religion and
science. 4. History (Theology) I. Title.
B4051.D61D66213  1997

                                           96-46720
                                           CIP

This is volume 1 in the continuing series
The Collected Works of Herman Dooyeweerd
Series B, Volume 1 ISBN 0-7734-8732-8
CWHD Series ISBN 0-7734-8731-X

*(The Collected Works comprise an A-Series and a B-Series)*

A CIP catalog record for this book is available from the British Library.

    The Edwin Mellen Press          The Edwin Mellen Press
          Box 450                      Box 67
      Lewiston, New York          Queenston, Ontario
      USA 14092-0450            CANADA L0S 1L0

                  The Edwin Mellen Press, Ltd.
                  Lampeter, Ceredigion, Wales
              UNITED KINGDOM SA48 8LT

            Printed in the United States of America

# Translators and Editors
## Christian Philosophy and the Meaning of History

Under the above title this volume brings together the following four separately titled essays by Herman Dooyeweerd:

1) "Christian Philosophy: An Exploration." This essay constitutes chapter I, *Calvinistische wijsbegeerte*, in *Verkenningen* (Buijten & Schipperheijn, Amsterdam, 1962 – pp.11-66). It first appeared in *Scientia* (W. de Haan, Zeist, 1956, pp.127-159).
Translator: *John Vriend*
Editors: *T. Grady Spires, Natexa Verbrugge*

2) "The Meaning of History." *De Zin der Geschiedenis*, from: *De Zin der Geschiedenis*, edited by J.D. Bierens de Haan et.al., Van Gorcum & Comp. N.V., Assen, 1942, pp.17-27.
Translators: *K.C. and A.L. Sewell*
Editor: *Magnus Verbrugge*

3) "The Criteria of Progressive and Reactionary Tendencies in History." An address delivered to the *Koninglijke Akademie van Wetenschappen* (Royal Academy of Sciences and Humanities), Amsterdam on the occasion of its 150th anniversary in 1958. First published simultaneously in Dutch, French and English by the Academy and now edited and re-published in English in this Volume with the permission of the Academy. [*Maatstaven ter onderkenning van progressieve en reactionaire bewegingen in de historische ontwikkeling.* Verslag van de plechtige viering van het honderdvijftigjarig bestaan der Koninklijke Nederlandse Akademie van Wetenschappen, 6-9 Mei 1958, pp.61-77; *Mouvements progressifs et régressifs dans l'histoire*, pp.139-154. *The criteria of progressive and reactionary tendencies in history*, pp.213-228; Amsterdam, N.V. Noord-Hollandse Uitgeversmaatschappij, 1958 {1959}.]
Editor: *Magnus Verbrugge*

4) "The dangers of the intellectual disarmament of Christianity in Science." This essay constitutes chapter IV, *De gevaren van de geestelijke ontwapening der Christenheid op het gebied van de Wetenschap* in the volume entitled *Geestelijk Weerloos of Weerbaar?* (Intellectually Defenceless or Armored?), introduced by J.H. DeGoede Jr., Ed. (Publisher not identified, Amsterdam, 1937, pp. 153-212).
Translator: *John Vriend*
Editors: *T. Grady Spires, Natexa Verbrugge, Magnus Verbrugge*

# Table of Contents

# Foreword

With the publication of this volume The Dooyeweerd Centre for Christian Philosophy continues the project of translating, editing and publishing the *Collected Works* of Herman Dooyeweerd, formerly carried on by The Herman Dooyeweerd Foundation.

The publication of the *Collected Works* will reflect the three dimensions of an integral Christian philosophical approach to science and scholarship. These can be identified as: (i) taking the history of philosophy fully into consideration, (ii) engaging in systematic philosophical reflection and (iii) interacting with the various academic disciplines in order to ascertain the special scientific fruitfulness of the former two tasks.

The publication project will differentiate into two separate series – each of which comprising all three dimensions mentioned above:

– Series A will contain multi-volume works as well as larger single volumes, each to be bound in a standard format.

– Series B, which will contain smaller volumes and volumes consisting of related articles, essays, speeches, and other material, each to be bound in a standard format.

In this Volume 1 of Series B a number of related articles are brought together. The first one provides the reader with a suitable introduction to Dooyeweerd's philosophy through the gateway of his own lucid remarks about the historical context and development of this new Christian philosophy and a clear exposition of its critique of the belief in the autonomy of theoretical thought, prevalent in so many projects of modernity. His subsequent brief analysis of the basic motives operative in the continuous unfolding of Western civilization adds depth and weight to the challenge this philosophy poses towards many schools of philosophy which are still unwilling to give an account of the deepest motivations of their activities.

The second chapter, dealing with *the meaning of history*, reveals a crucial facet of Dooyeweerd's systematic philosophy. His entire analysis of the historical opening-up process sees in the historical aspect the *nodal point* of all *meaning disclosure* – guided by the *function of faith*. The meaning of history is treated within the broader context of many systematic distinctions drawn from his philosophy in general.

The third chapter, discussing the *criteria of progressive and reactionary tendencies in history*, appropriately supplements this analysis of the meaning of history, since it sets out to unveil the fundamental principles which guide all historical change and which help us to discern both normative and antinormative historical events.

By pointing to the conflicts and dialectical tensions that occur in the process of the opening-up of human culture – which result from the absolutization of what is relative – Dooyeweerd does not hesitate to underline the biblical revelation that the only path leading away from the spirit of apostasy underlying every absolutization is given in the awareness that there would be no future hope for the entire process of cultural development "if Jesus Christ had not become the center of world history."

What is only touched on in this third article is Dooyeweerd's truly original theory of modal aspects – along with his theory of "individuality-structures" (accounting for our experience of concrete events, processes and societal relationships) – a unique contribution to the legacy of western philosophy. The most appropriate orientation to his philosophy will be found in the yet to be published *Introduction to Legal Science*, written by himself. That *Introduction* is actually an introduction to his philosophy as such.

The fourth and final chapter deals with a reality still confronting Christianity today, namely *the dangers of the intellectual disarmament of Christianity in science and scholarship*. The devastating effects inherent in both the accommodation of un-biblical motives by *Roman Catholicism* and the secularization of Christianity by modern *Humanism* are treated with a penetrating analytical profundity. According to Dooyeweerd one should add to the dualism of faith and science thus established the generally uncritical acceptance of the *separation* between philosophy and the special sciences that had developed in humanistic thought. With historical sensitivity he also realizes that science and scholarship indeed function in our Western culture as a major *spiritual* power of our day.

Dooyeweerd shows how tragic it is that humanism managed to acquire its historical power to shape scientific development partly thanks to a centuries-long attempt at accommodation and synthesis on the part of Christian thought itself. The all-pervasive import of a radical biblical starting-point in science and scholarship finds an ample expression in the final statement of this last essay of this volume:

*All Christians who in their scientific work are ashamed of the Name of Christ Jesus, because they desire honor among people, will be totally useless in the mighty struggle to recapture science,* one of the great powers of Western culture, for the Kingdom of God. This struggle is not hopeless, however, so long as it is waged in the full armour of faith in Him who has said "All authority in heaven and on earth has been given to Me," and again, "Take heart! I have overcome the world."

D.F.M. Strauss
General editor

# Christian Philosophy: An Exploration[1]

## Introduction

THE TERM "Calvinistic Philosophy," used to describe the philosophical movement which has been developing around "The Philosophy of the Cosmonomic Idea" since the nineteen thirties, may in many respects cause misunderstanding.

The term can only be explained historically by the fact that this movement originated in the calvinistic revival which toward the end of the previous century, led to renewed reflection on the relation of the Christian religion to science, culture, and society. Abraham Kuyper, under whose inspiring leadership this new reflection took place, pointed out that the great movement of the Reformation could not continue to be restricted to the reformation of the church and theology. Its biblical point of departure touched the religious root of the whole of temporal life and had to assert its validity in all of its sectors. Kuyper found that insight into these implications had been best expressed by Calvin, and so for lack of a better term began to speak of "Calvinism" as an all-embracing world view which was clearly distinguishable from both Roman Catholicism and Humanism.

Kuyper was very much aware of the objections that could be raised against this term. For instance, it could easily lead to the misunderstanding that a particular theological system was being canonized, giving Calvin's thought an authority which in the biblical-reformational view can never be ascribed to a human being. At the same time this would imply a dubious narrowing of the basis for discussion, one that had to detract from the universal, indeed *ecumenical* or catholic, significance of this perspective, and lead inevitably to the formation of Christian sects.

Kuyper forcefully rejected this misunderstanding. Experience has since demonstrated that the pejorative term "Calvinism" is widely viewed as a label for the formation of a specific group, a label which ob-

---

1  This essay constitutes chapter I in *Verkenningen* ("Calvinistische Wijsbegeerte"), Buijten & Schipperheijn, Amsterdam 1962. It first appeared in 1956 in *Scientia* (W. de Haan, Zeist, 1956, pp.127-159). Translator: *John Vriend*; Editors: *T. Grady Spires, Natexa Verbrugge.*

1

scures rather than clarifies the true intentions of the Reformational movement to which it refers.

For what did Kuyper mean when he again brought out in the open the reformational principle which animated Calvin and which he taught was life-embracing? What moved him, against every dualistic division between a "Christian" and "worldly" domain, to call for recognition of the universal Kingship of Christ in all areas of life?

His deepest concern was for a life and thought rooted in the central unity of Holy Scripture which is above the divergence of human ideas and interpretations. It is above them because it does not proceed from the human being but rather, as the spiritual driving force (*dynamis*) of the divine Word, takes *possession* of a person and demands unconditional self-surrender. The central operation of that spiritual dynamis affects the human heart, by attraction or by repulsion, prior to any theoretical reflection of the human mind. The possessive grip on the heart of human existence must be imparted from this central base to every orientation of thought and life.

The focus of concern here is not just the individual but the fellowship of the new community rooted in Christ; it is the kingdom of God which is restlessly at war with the kingdom of darkness. The whole world in all of its varying sectors is the arena for this struggle, a struggle which spreads out from its religious root in the human heart to the whole of life in time.

God has not abandoned his creation to the spirit of apostasy. The creation is His. It is subject to His absolute sovereignty. For that reason the central dynamic grip of the Word of God affects not only the personal life of the Christian, nor only the church as an institutional fellowship, but all human social relationships, politics, culture, science, and philosophy.

The recognition of the radical[1] and integral significance of the Christian religion should not be presented as a specifically calvinistic point of view. Rather, the significance of the Christian religion irresistibly forces itself upon us from within the central ground-motive[2] of Holy Scripture: that of creation, fall, and redemption through Christ Jesus in the fellowship of the Holy Spirit. When that acknowledgement makes way for the acceptance of an "autonomy" of the "natural" or "worldly" life, it is exclusively due to the influence of unbiblical motives.

Kuyper penetrated beyond the theological and philosophical issues of the day to the deepest and absolutely central spiritual forces that set hu-

---

1  *Editorial note* (DFMS): See the explanation of the term *radical* in the Glossary.
2  *Editorial note* (DFMS): See the explanation of this expression in the *Glossary* (p.112).

man life and thought in motion. These forces cannot be considered to be on the level of theoretical or scientific problems, because all theoretical reflection is already in their grip before it gets under way. These central spiritual ground-motives are disclosed in their true nature only when a person is inwardly transformed by the Word in which God reveals himself to human beings and leads them to the discovery of themselves.

In the aggravation, the *scandal ("skandalon")* of this disclosure, which culminates in the cross of Golgotha, is revealed the crisis of an unavoidable conflict between the spirit of apostasy and the spiritual dynamis of the Word of God which exposes everyone. Here, in the utterly central sphere of religion, the final antithesis becomes manifest, one that demands an unavoidable choice of position in the life and thought of a person.

By following Abraham Kuyper in this purely biblical line of thought, the philosophy of the cosmonomic idea accepts that by virtue of the central, radical, and integral ground-motive of Holy Scripture (i.e., that of creation-fall-redemption by Christ Jesus, the Incarnate Word), "the key of knowledge" is not dependent on human beings; instead, it takes command over them. Its radical spiritual meaning is directly revealed to humankind by operation of the Holy Spirit and not through the intermediary of a fallible theological exegesis of a number of Bible texts and of a system of theological dogmatics.

Knowledge of this radical meaning is a realization gained through confession, not a conclusion drawn as a result of theological reflection. For that reason this central motive can also be the actual *ecumenical* point of unification for all who, regardless of their denominational affiliation, live in the biblical spirit of the Reformation and take seriously the radical and integral grip of the Word of God upon the whole of temporal life. This is why Kuyper already took issue with the sectarian tendencies of ecclesiasticism in the great cultural struggle during his day. And, although he opposed "Romanism" in principle, he continued to be faithful to the Catholic Christian starting point which excludes no one from the *militia Christi* on account of their church affiliation.

## Prolegomena to the Philosophy of the Cosmonomic Idea

This brief introduction was necessary to put the spiritual background of the philosophy of the cosmonomic idea in proper perspective and to safeguard it from misconceptions to which it is exposed due to its infelicitous designation as "Calvinistic Philosophy." The fact that its adherents in various countries belong to divergent church traditions, and that there is an increasing sympathy for it among Roman Catholic thinkers who have been influenced by the so-called *new theology*, prove that its ecumenical Christian basis is no empty slogan.

This philosophy is not a closed system. It does not claim to have a monopoly on truth in the sphere of philosophical reflection, nor that the provisional conclusions of its inquiries have been made sacrosanct because of the central biblical motive which motivates and controls it. As a *philosophy* it does not in any way demand a privileged position for itself; on the contrary, it seeks to create a real basis for philosophical dialogue among the different movements – movements which often isolate themselves and which can only lead to stagnation and overestimation of one's own ideas. The "transcendental critique of theoretical thought," which is the key to understanding the philosophy of the cosmonomic idea, aims to serve the purpose of this dialogue. It is also the means by which this philosophy seeks to approach the diametrically opposed camps of philosophy in terms of their own respective deepest spiritual backgrounds.

In this essay, only a few *prolegomena* to the philosophy of the cosmonomic idea can be further pursued.

By a "transcendental critique of theoretical thought" this philosophy means a genuinely critical (i.e., unsparing of any single so-called philosophical axiom) inquiry into the universally valid conditions which make the theoretical attitude possible and which *are demanded by the intrinsic structure of the latter*. In this last qualification lies the fundamental difference between a "theologically-transcendent" and a "transcendental" critique – two kinds of critique to which one can subject philosophical thought. The first does not really touch the inner nature and intrinsic structure of the theoretical attitude of the human mind but only subjects the different results of philosophical thought to the test of Holy Scripture or of a church dogma that is thought to be infallible. This critique remains dogmatic, however, and is of no value to philosophy so long as the dogma of the autonomy of philosophy is not subjected to a genuinely transcendental critique and the inner point of contact between philosophy and religion is not laid bare. Besides, it is dangerous for theology when it does not take stock of its own philosophical presuppositions – presuppositions which it has all too often forced upon its scientific exegesis of Scripture without examining their roots. Just think of the influence of Greek and modern philosophical concepts on the theological understanding of the analogy of being, the relationship between soul and body, creation, time and eternity, causality, etc. The transcendental critique at which the philosophy of the cosmonomic idea aims is just as necessary for theology as it is for its ancient rival, philosophy.

This "transcendental critique" must not be confused with the "transcendental critique of knowledge" launched by Immanuel Kant [1724-

1807], nor with the transcendental-phenomenological critique of knowledge undertaken by Edmund Husserl [1859-1938]. The deepest impulse of Kant's thought took him, in his critical period, toward "practical metaphysics." He aimed to investigate only the limits and *a priori* conditions of scientific knowledge, limiting the latter, moreover, to the mathematical-physical, and rejecting its metaphysical claims. He believed that this theory of knowledge could determine these boundaries and conditions in a way that was universally valid. But the theory of knowledge itself did not become a critical problem for Kant. He assumed the autonomy of "theoretical reason" without having first undertaken a critical inquiry into the universally valid conditions of the theoretical attitude of thought itself.

This dogmatic starting point of Kant's theory of knowledge became the major obstacle for a genuinely critical posture. It prevented him from considering the fact that it is here, in the theory of knowledge itself, that the principal difference in starting point between the various schools manifests itself. It is a difference which precedes, *and controls,* all theoretical reflection.

The same applies, in even much greater measure, to Edmund Husserl's transcendental phenomenology, which he characterizes, in his *Cartesian Meditations*, as "critique of transcendental-phenomenological knowledge." This theory of knowledge, presenting itself as the "final critique of knowledge," goes much further than Kant's in its absolutization of the theoretical attitude. Kant at least still postulated a "Primacy of Practical Reason" and wanted to set principal limits to "Theoretical Reason." The fact that Kant's *Critique of Practical Reason* remained bound in principle to the theoretical attitude does not detract from the fact that he remained fully conscious of the dependence of his critique of practical reason on a faith which, however much he wanted to keep it within the bounds of autonomous reason, was, nevertheless, inaccessible to a *purely* theoretical approach.

Even this critical reserve with respect to the theoretical attitude is fundamentally abolished in Husserl's phenomenology. In Husserl, the faith of Kant's practical reason is subjected to theoretical phenomenological reduction (ἐποχή), as belonging to a pre-critical, "natural life attitude." In this connection phenomenologists believe that, though they themselves are independent of any faith in carrying out their research, they can grasp all the essentials of the intentional act of faith in theoretical contemplation and expose the transcendental constitution of all possible belief-content by a purely theoretical method.

Here the absolutization of the theoretical attitude is in fact no longer counterbalanced by any sort of critical reserve. It is for this very reason that Husserl's "transcendental" phenomenological critique of knowledge forms an extremely promising field of study for a radical transcendental critique of thought which will force the phenomenological critique to pose as a transcendental problem the very autonomy of the phenomenological attitude which it has accepted as an axiom.

How can one explain that the Aristotelian theory of knowledge leads to very different results from those of Locke and Hume, and that the critique of knowledge of the latter two again deviates fundamentally from that of Kant or from the phenomenological one of Husserl? What was at issue here? Was it merely a purely theoretical reflection on the nature and conditions of the theoretical process, a reflection which steadily deepens and corrects itself in the course of history in its confrontation with the advancing results of science?

This interpretation is accepted by all who proceed axiomatically from the autonomy of philosophical theoretical thought. For them the possibility of scientific philosophical debate stands or falls with the acceptance or rejection of the "axiom" of autonomy. Even existentialist philosophy, at least in its non-Christianized expression, did not challenge the autonomy of philosophy, even though it did direct philosophy toward a totally different plane of thought than that of reflection on the limits and conditions of scientific knowledge or that of a non-existential phenomenology.

But, to someone with a truly critical attitude of thought, the mere fact that a more precise definition of this autonomy would disclose major conceptual differences must militate against acceptance of the self-sufficiency of philosophical thought as an axiom. This axiom, too, must be posed as a problem for a genuinely *radical* transcendental critique of thought.

All philosophy, in distinction from practical wisdom, remains bound to the theoretical attitude. This attitude is by no means identical with the so-called objectivizing, or (to use the idiom of existentialism) "factual" attitude, which focuses only on "that which is present." The truth is, rather, that these "givens," in their typical antithetical position toward the intrinsically "historical" existence of humans themselves, only assume in the theoretical attitude the peculiar configuration that existentialism has given to them.

The theoretical attitude of thought does not disclose its inner nature and structure until it is juxtaposed to the pre-theoretical attitude of naive experience. The first, in distinction from the second, is characterized by the antithetic relation in which the logical aspect of the act of thought (the analytical) confronts the non-logical aspects of the horizon of human experience.

6

As a result, the non-logical aspects, standing as they do in an antithetic relation to the human analytical function, *resist* the effort to separate them from each other by human logic and to grasp them conceptually. From this resistance arises the theoretical problem.

In this "antithetic relation" there is not hidden an opposition between subject and object as such, since it rather concerns a theoretical opposition of the logical aspect to the non-logical aspects of one and the same temporal horizon of human experience. These aspects are merely the modes in which we experience temporal reality. They form a coherent framework of modalities which belongs to the structure of the human horizon of experience. As such the framework is basic to all empirical reality in time as an *a priori* datum of its intrinsic diversity of meaning. Confusion between these modal aspects and the empirical phenomena that appear in them in our experience has frequently blocked insight into the nature of the "antithetic relation of thought" (the Gegenstand relation).

This is also the reason why philosophy has paid almost no attention to the real modal structures of the aspects of experience. No one should think, however, that these modal aspects are only a construction of the philosophy of the cosmonomic idea and that other schools of thought are therefore free to ignore them. The modal aspects of our experience will not let themselves be ignored by the critical theoretical attitude of thought, for they confer on experience the primary diversity of meaning which is basic to all theoretical distinction and makes it possible. In the final analysis, it is these modal aspects that determine the distinct areas of investigation of the special sciences, although within this framework the special sciences can, of course, further specialize in many ways.

For it is not the empirical phenomena in their totality which can offer a criterion for the delimitation of these areas of scientific study. The very same phenomena which physics investigates in terms of the operation of physical energy are considered by biologists under the aspect of organic life. For the science of history, these phenomena may take on a historical aspect. Just think of the historical significance of natural catastrophes like floods, or the influence of the Russian winter on the course of Napoleon's campaign in Russia, and so on. Economics views them in terms of the economic aspect. Jurisprudence will study them under the juridical aspect of objective facts of law in their necessary bearing on subjective legal relationships. Aesthetics will analyze them from *its* perspective – consider the aesthetics of colors and of sound waves.

In philosophy, differences can only arise with respect to the question of how one should view the mutual interrelation and coherence of these modal aspects and, in this connection, how they may be distinguished theoretically. But the modal diversity of the horizon of our experience itself is an undeniable state of affairs, and every attempt in philosophy to escape the force of this state of affairs only leads to confused concepts and theories devoid of all genuine specificity of meaning. For that reason every philosophical view of the horizon of human experience, and the reality which offers itself within that horizon, must immediately be tested by the modal dimension of that horizon. Every form of reduction of the modal diversity of the aspects of experience necessarily leads to theoretically confused statements of the problem and becomes a real snare in the philosophical argument.

In the philosophical, theoretical attitude of thought, every totality embracing a variety of aspects within itself necessarily turns into a theoretical problem. And, *no matter how the problem is posed in detail*, it always implies the theoretical Gegenstand relation in the transcendental sense explained above. For that reason, insight into this transcendental relation is a primary condition for a transcendental critique of philosophical reflection. Precisely because this reflection, being theoretical in nature, is possible only *in* the modal diversity of the aspects of experience, every synoptic theoretical perspective on things necessarily has to make its way through this dimension of the horizon of our experience, while giving a theoretical exposition of this totality. Such a theoretical synopsis also gives to the transcendental critique of thought an account of its *content* and *meaning*. And the mere fact that all philosophical terms become multivocal whenever we try to bypass the task of distinguishing modal aspects theoretically – which is only possible in the "Gegenstand relation" – shows that this transcendental relation is a structural condition of philosophical thought.

### The First Transcendental Problem

Now, the first transcendental problem with which the antithetic structure of the theoretical attitude confronts us may initially be defined as follows:

*Does the theoretical antithesis between the logical aspect and the non-logical modes of our experience correspond to the integral structure of the horizon of our experience and hence the structure of empirical reality?*

If this were so, then any possibility of a logical distinction between non-logical aspects and, with it, the possibility of the theoretical attitude itself, would be cancelled. The logical aspect of our thought would be separated by an unbridgeable chasm from the non-logical modes of our experience. Nor would there be any room left for the pre-theoretical attitude of naive experience.

In naive experience, too, we are actively thinking. Human experience is not a matter of undergoing, and reacting to, stimuli in animal fashion. It presupposes a combination of ego-related acts of reception and response in which the activity of thought plays an essential role. So long as this act-life has not developed in a person, that person lacks the possibility of *experience*.

But the naive attitude of thought differs in principle from the theoretical. The former is devoid of any trace of antithetic structure and, for that reason, does not know of any theoretical problems. In naive experience we are embedded, with our analytical function as well as with all the other modal functions of our experiencing consciousness and sub-consciousness, right in the midst of empirical reality. Here we grasp reality in the typical totality-structures of individual things, concrete events, concrete social relationships, etc., in which all modal aspects are typically individualized and integrated in unbroken coherence, grouped together as a whole without any analytical distinction between the modal aspects themselves.[1]

The naive formation of concepts is not directed to these modal aspects but to things, events, etc., as *individual totalities*; it is not, for example, oriented toward abstract numerical or spatial relations or toward the operations of energy, but toward countable, spatial, and working realities, in whose empirical totality-structure the logical aspect is bound in unbreakable coherence with the non-logical modalities of experience. All these aspects are *implicitly* experienced in relation to things and events as integral entities, and not *explicitly* as they would be in consequence of distinguishing them theoretically. But how is this possible?

This is possible only by virtue of the *subject-object relation* which is characteristic of naive experience, a relation which therefore has to differ fundamentally from the theoretical Gegenstand relation with which it is continually equated in epistemological theory.

In this subject-object relation we ascribe to things and events an object-function in those modal aspects of the horizon of our experience in which they cannot possibly function as subject.

Naive experience makes a distinction between subject-functions and object-functions. For instance, it knows very well that water by itself is not alive, but that it still has an essential object-function in the biotic modality as a vital "means of life." It knows very well that a bird's nest by itself is not the subject of life but that it fulfills an essential objective function in the life of the bird. It knows that a church building cannot be

---

1  The transcendental investigation of these individuality structures is, next to that of the modal structures, certainly the most important positive part of the philosophy of the cosmonomic idea.

a subject in the aspect of faith but that it nevertheless serves an objective purpose in the worship of a faith-community, a purpose which comes to objective expression in the structure of the building itself. Furthermore, these subject-object relations are grasped, in naive experience, as structural relations within empirical reality itself. At no time are the object-functions of things *absolutized* and attributed to a so-called "thing-in-it-self" (*Ding an sich*). On the contrary, object-functions are experienced in unbreakable relation to possible subject-functions in the aspects concerned. For instance, under normal lighting a particular rose may have the objective sensory color "red" to all normal human perception. A thing has objective-analytical characteristics in relation to subjective human concept formation. A work of art has a (*qualifying*) objective aesthetic function, both as the objective expression of a subjective aesthetic conception of the artist and in relation to the subjective aesthetic appreciation of the viewer.

As a result of these subject-object relations we experience reality at once, in the total coherence of the differing modal aspects of the horizon of our experience. Naive experience leaves the structures of empirical experience intact. Though it does not understand these aspects explicitly in a conceptual way, it does have an implicit *awareness* of them.

The antithetic theoretical attitude, on the other hand, *breaks up* reality, in the diversity of its modal aspects, *even if the theoretical thinker, lacking insight into the nature of the antithetic relation, is not conscious of it.* Epistemology finds itself in this antithetical attitude of thought when it tries to set the subject and object of knowledge *in opposition to* each other, thus in fact setting the logical aspect of thought up against a non-logical aspect of human experience (that of sensory perception). And the so-called phenomena of nature function of course only as object, albeit in unbreakable relation to subjective sensory observation. Counting, measuring and weighing, as applied by the exact sciences, can only bring the objectivity of the observed phenomena to light in inseparable connection with possible subjective acts of counting, measuring, and weighing, acts which occur within the integral horizon of human experience. But the objective countability, measurability, and weighability of these phenomena already constitute an appeal to modal aspects of our experience other than that of sensory perception. The theoretical picture of reality is always the product of theoretical abstraction. Precisely what is abstracted from the structure of experienced reality is that which is one of its first pre-conditions, viz., the continuous bond of coherence between the logical aspect and the non-logical aspects.

In the nature of things, this theoretical abstraction cannot *really* cancel out this bond. The *real* act of thought does not function only in the logical modality but equally as much in the other modal aspects of the horizon of our experience, and in the unbreakable coherence of these modal functions. In other words, the antithetic relation only bears an *intentional* character. It is posited within the real act of thought the moment we direct our analytical function toward one or more non-analytical aspects of our experience, aspects which we abstract for that purpose from the inter-modal synthesis of the horizon of our experience.

Every scientific discipline does this when it seeks to investigate empirical reality from a specific point of view. But in this investigation it does not focus its theoretical attention upon the modal structure of such an aspect itself; rather, it focuses on the coherence of the actual phenomena which function within that structure. Where they are grasped only in certain specific, abstract aspects, these phenomena no longer come into view in their integral reality but only in terms of specific modal functions.

But philosophy too, though not characterized by the particular research-attitude of the special sciences, remains bound, in all of its possible nuances and schools, to the theoretical attitude. It cannot remain in the attitude of naive experience, because the real philosophical problems arise only within the theoretical attitude. Therefore, the first transcendental basic problem which the theoretical attitude poses can now be definitively formulated as follows: *what do we abstract in the intentional antithetic thought-relation from the integral structure of the horizon of our experience?*

By dogmatically proceeding from it, the adherents of the dogma of the autonomy of theoretical thought remained unaware of this fundamental problem. They equated the *antithetical relation* of theoretical thought with the *subject-object relation,* and so arrived at a curious deformation of naive experience seen as a kind of theory. Naive experience was now itself interpreted as a theory about reality, the so-called naive-realistic one. According to naive realism, the human mind was situated over against objective reality like a camera, and reality *an sich* (in itself, apart from the conscious human mind) was faithfully reflected in sensory observation. This naive-realistic theory of naive experience was alleged to have been thoroughly refuted by the Kantian theory of knowledge in its alliance with modern physics.

This is indeed a peculiar interpretation of the attitude of naive experience! But it makes sense in light of the absolutization of the theoretical antithetic relation, which already in Greek metaphysics led to a process in which the theorizing, analytical faculty of the human mind became autonomous, and whose Object (Gegenstand) became "a reality in and by itself." Indeed, the de-theorizing of the interpretation of naive experience is a *conditio sine qua non* for a transcendental critique of theoretical thought.

To the question formulated earlier, namely, what is abstracted in the antithetic thought-relation from the integral structure of the horizon of our experience, the answer of the philosophy of the cosmonomic idea is: *the inter-modal coherence of time*. Time is here taken in a fully universal sense, a sense to which neither Husserl's "phenomenological time" nor existentialism's "existential-historical time" corresponds. Time in the sense intended here, i.e., in its inter-modal continuity, is not at all open to theoretical penetration, because it *precedes* every theoretical distinction as its ultimate transcendental premise. We experience time as something that does not exhaust itself in the unbroken stream of subjective experiences. Universal time envelopes all the modal aspects of the horizon of our experience; it expresses itself in each of these modes in the specific meaning of that modality but exhausts itself in none of them. The mathematical aspect of quantity and that of spatiality are intrinsically as *temporal* as the mathematical aspect of pure movement, and as the physical, biotic, psychical, logical, cultural-historical aspects, or that of symbolic meaning. But integral time has a continuous depth-dimension which reaches beyond the modal boundaries of the aspects of experience and brings the latter into an unbreakable coherence of meaning. But then how is theoretical philosophical reflection on this universal time possible? Is not the fact that the philosophy of the cosmonomic idea involves universal time in its theorizing a denial of the position that time is not open to theoretical penetration?

Clearly the answer can only be that in the theoretical attitude of thought we can approach universal time only in a theoretical survey of its modal aspects as these are distinguished in this theoretical attitude. In that case, we approach it in the necessary theoretical discontinuity of a theoretical idea of a totality which continues to appeal to an intuitive sense of its continuity in the attitude of naive experience, but keeps us from equating time with one of its modal manifestations, e.g. the continuous sense of its duration in the physical sphere, the continuity of time in history, the biotic continuity of living things in process of development or the continuity of movement.

Integral time manifests itself in each of its modal aspects in unbreakable correlation with the *order* as well as the *duration* of time, the second being subject to the first. Order is the law-side, duration is the subject-side (or the subjective-objective side) of time. The irrationalistic (subjectivistic) view of time which identifies true time with the subjective duration of it, as it manifests itself in the biotic or the psychical or the historic modalities, is just as much grounded in a meaningless theoretical absolutization as the rationalistic (objectivistic) view which interprets time as the mathematical ordering of movement and relates it to a supposedly absolute *objective time*, without sensing that the subject-object relation renders meaningless every absolutization of an objective (duration of) time in the modality of movement. All such views of time are assumed to grasp time in its integral inter-modal continuity. But in a genuinely transcendental-critical attitude we begin to realize that, in order to bring all fundamental modes of time openly into view, one has to abstract them from this inter-modal continuity.

All transcendental structures in which we experience reality within the universal horizon of time – both the modal structures of the aspects and the typical totality-structures of individuality – are intrinsically temporal.[1] They are grounded in the universal order of time in its intrinsic relatedness to the duration of time. Theoretical thought remains enclosed entirely within this temporal horizon. Theoretically we can abstract the transcendental time structures from all actual time duration. In doing this we can create the illusion that we have incorporated timeless structures in our theoretical perspective. In fact, these are abstracted *temporal* structures and the process of theoretical abstraction itself remains enclosed within the universal horizon of time which made it possible in the first place.

In the theoretical attitude we cannot, of course, be satisfied with and stop at the theoretical antithesis between the logical and the non-logical aspects in the Gegenstand relation. We cannot stand still in the face of a theoretical *problem*. We must proceed from the theoretical *antithesis* to the theoretical *synthesis* to arrive at a theoretical concept of the non-analytical aspects. It may be that in the special sciences this synthesis occurs only implicitly because there all theoretic attention is directed to the coherence of data (reality functions) which offer themselves for study within the abstracted *Gegenstand* field. But philosophy, if it is to remain in fact critical, has to arrive at an explicitly theoretical concept of the distinguished, that is, analytically set apart, modal aspects of the temporal horizon of our experience in order to be able to grasp them in an all encompassing theory. It cannot escape this totality perspective because every aspect of that horizon of experience contained in the antithetic relation displays a foundational modal structure in which an inner coherence with all other modal aspects comes to expression. It is only in the inter-modal coherence that the modal aspects reveal their own inner nature, and, although in the theoretical attitude of thought we are compelled to abstract them from the continuity of that coherence, this conti-

1 *Editorial note* (DFMS): Compare the Glossary remarks on "individuality-structure."

nuity forces itself on us even in the theoretical discontinuity of the abstracted aspects.

The special sciences themselves are forced to account for that coherence because the aspects, which in principle determine their field of inquiry, reflect and relate to one another. The fundamental elementary concepts of these sciences display a reciprocal connectedness despite the fact that in each scientific area they take on a special modal qualification. And when the special sciences appeal to empirical reality to establish their theoretical positions, their appeal is not to empirical reality as it presents itself in naive experience but to a reality as seen through the spectacles of a theoretical view of the whole. Here the often unconscious philosophical presuppositions of special scientific research manifest themselves, presuppositions which need to be brought into the open in a radically critical critique of thought.

## The Second Transcendental Problem

The inter-modal synthesis on which theoretical thought depends gives rise to a second transcendental basic problem, which can be formulated as follows: *from what standpoint can the aspects of our horizon of experience, which were set apart and in opposition to each other in the theoretical antithesis, be reunited in a theoretical synthesis?*

By raising this second basic problem, every possible starting point of theoretic thought is subjected to a transcendental critique. And here it must finally become evident whether the presupposed autonomy of theoretic thought is grounded in the inner nature and structure of this thought or whether it is rather a supra-theoretical prejudgment. If the latter proves to be the case, then transcendental critique may not rest until it has brought to light the true nature of this prejudgment.

Now it is at once obvious that the true starting point of theoretical synthesis, however it may have been chosen, is in no case to be found in one of the terms of the antithetic relation. It must necessarily *transcend* the theoretical antithesis to be able to function as the central point of reference for the synthesis; that is, to be able to relate the modal diversity of the aspects of our experience to a deeper radical unity of our consciousness, one that is fundamental to every act of thought. This is certain: the antithetic relation, with which the theoretical attitude stands or falls (because all theoretical problems originate there) does not in itself offer a bridge between the logical aspect of thought and its non-logical *Gegenstand*-aspects. A purely logical synthesis is something other than the inter-modal synthesis at stake in the second transcendental basic problem of the critique of thought. Nor can time, considered in its inter-modal continuity, serve as the sought-after central point of reference for the synthesis, for no other reason than that it cannot be a point of reference for the theoretical antithesis.

Already at this stage the dogma of the autonomy of theoretical thought seems to lead its adherents into an inescapable impasse. In order to maintain the self-sufficiency of the theoretical attitude, they have little or no choice but to adopt the conclusion that their starting point is to be found in theoretic thought itself. For philosophy this means that the sole starting point for a theoretical total view of the horizon of our experience, and the empirical reality which presents itself within it, would have to be sought within this thought itself. In the philosophy of the cosmonomic idea this view is called the *immanence standpoint* and every philosophy which thinks it is able to adhere to it is described as *immanence philosophy*.

But theoretical thought, by virtue of its intentional antithetic structure, is dependent on inter-modal synthesis. There are as many modalities of theoretical synthesis possible as there are non-logical aspects in our horizon of experience. There is synthetic theoretical thought of a mathematical, physical, biological, psychological, historical, linguistic, aesthetic, economic, juridical, moral-theoretical and other nature. In which of these possible special scientific viewpoints will the philosopher's total view seek its starting point? Regardless of the choice made, it will always turn out to be the *absolutization* of a specific synthetically grasped modal aspect of the horizon of human experience. This is the source of all the *isms* in the theoretical view of reality, isms which continually strive to reduce all, or at least some, of the remaining aspects to modalities of the one that has been absolutized, isms which play their confusing role both in philosophy and in the special sciences (in their appeal to reality).

Now such isms (like energism, biologism, psychologism, historicism, etc.) are uncritical in a double sense. In the first place, they can never be theoretically justified.

The theoretical antithesis resists every attempt to reduce one of the abstracted modal aspects to another, and it avenges the absolutization by entangling the theoretical thought which is guilty of it in internal antinomies. In the entire horizon of time embraced by the theoretical attitude, there is simply no room for the absolute. And a theoretical inter-modal synthesis cannot be detached from the theoretical antithetic relation which is its prerequisite.

Here we touch upon the second reason for the uncritical nature of the different isms. In each of them the problem concerning the starting point of the theoretical synthesis returns unsolved. Since it cannot derive its origin from theoretical thought itself such an absolutization suggests the influence of a supra-theoretical starting point which controls the theoretical view of the mutual interrelation and coherence of the modal aspects of experience which have been theoretically set apart.

Immanence philosophy will always attempt to escape the force of the antithetic relation which threatens the autonomy of the philosophical attitude of thought. The attempt takes many forms.

It can try by seeking refuge in an irrationalistic metaphysics of life, in which all static concepts are replaced by fluid ones able to express vital movement as grasped in the immediate, mobile forms of intuition.

It can try in the way of "eidetic" phenomenology which believes it can, by applying methodical phenomenological "reductions" (ἐποχή), grasp the essential structures of the totality as given in intentional acts of consciousness by an immediate intuitive observation of nature.

It can also try the path of existential phenomenology which, like the philosophy of life, disassociates itself expressly from "objectivizing" thought. It takes its starting point in the concrete situation of being "thrown into the world" of historical existence and, in the phenomenological analysis of the existential moods of "care" and "dread," rejects the Husserlian method of reduction; and in so doing believes it is escaping theoretical abstraction in the process.

Over against these modern philosophical movements the transcendental critique of theoretical thought undertaken by the philosophy of the cosmonomic idea seems to fail, insofar as it posits that the theoretical abstraction implied in the antithetic relation is an essential feature of the theoretical attitude. But this is mere illusion. All the philosophical movements referred to expressly disassociate themselves from the attitude of naive experience. This very act of disassociation already implies the antithetic relation in the sense intended by the philosophy of the cosmonomic idea. It is the covert absolutization of theoretical abstraction which creates the illusion that philosophical reflection has immediate access to the integral temporal horizon of human experience. The transcendental critique of theoretical thought disturbs this illusion by bringing the hidden absolutization to light.

In this critique, the inescapable problem of the interrelation and coherence of the fundamental modal aspects of the horizon of human experience plays an essential role. This problem can never be obviated by operating with theoretically untested total views of "life," "stream of consciousness," "world," "existence," etc., nor by reducing the integral horizon of experience to its sensual and logical aspects, because in their respective modal structures both refer to all other modalities.

Meanwhile, it would certainly be premature and incorrect to suppose that the immanence standpoint would necessarily have to lead to an absolutization of a specific scientific point of view or to one single absolutization. It is the task of the transcendental critique of thought to investigate all the possibilities it offers for a transcendental-philosophical investigation of the structure of the horizon of human experience, because this investigation is necessarily implied in the transcendental critique of the theoretical attitude. It is for this reason that in the course of this critique the philosophy of the cosmonomic idea paid special attention to the critical transcendental philosophy of Immanuel Kant, the transcendental phenomenology of Edmund Husserl and other transcendental movements in immanence philosophy.

Kant most certainly discerned the uncritical character of the absolutization of a special theoretical synthesis. He was aware of the necessity of a central reference point for all synthetic acts of thought. He nonetheless believed he could identify in theoretical reason such a starting point that would be at the base of every possible theoretical synthesis and therefore not obtained by the absolutization of a specific scientific viewpoint.

According to the philosopher at Konigsberg, to discover this immanent starting point in which all synthetic acts of thought converge in a deeper central unity, one has to look away from the concrete object (Gegenstand) on which theoretical thought focuses and take the road of critical theoretical self-reflection. And, indeed, this road offers great promise. For, ignoring for the moment Kant's neglect of the real antithetical relation and noting the great diversity of modal aspects in which the horizon of human experience seems to diverge, one cannot deny that, so long as philosophical thought in its logical function continues to be directed to the opposed modal aspects of human experience which form its Gegenstand, it will dissipate itself in this theoretical diversity of modalities. Only when it is directed toward the thinking self does it gain a concentric focus on the unity of a consciousness which must lie at the base of all the diversity of the aspects of experience.

Ask all the disciplines which work in the domain of anthropology: "what is a human being?" and you will get a sampling of data and attributes which relate to specific aspects of human existence. But the question "what is the human being it-*self* in the unity of its selfhood?" cannot be answered by all the sciences put together. Human selfhood functions, to be sure, in all the modal aspects of the temporal horizon of human experience but it is nonetheless a *root-unity* which simultaneously *transcends* all these aspects.

So the way of critical self-reflection is in fact the only one that can lead to a discovery of the true starting point of a theoretical synthesis. Socrates already knew this when he made the Delphic maxim "know thyself" the primary requirement for critical philosophical reflection.

## The Third Transcendental Problem

But this gives rise to a new transcendental problem which can be formulated as follows: *how is this critical self-reflection, this concentric direction of theoretical thought toward the self, possible, and what is its origin?*

There can be no doubt that this third problem is also forced on us by the inner, intentional structure of the theoretical attitude. This is evident when we remember that theoretical thought itself is bound to the theoretical diversity of the modalities of experience even when it directs its attention to the experience of totality within the horizon of time. This problem is not solved by the distinction between a so-called reflexive and an objective kind of theoretical thought, the first referring back to the thinking subject, while the second focuses upon actual objects. At stake now is not the subject-object relation in human thought, but the antithetic relation in its fundamental transcendental theoretical sense. So long as the so-called thinking subject is locked in the Gegenstand relation, it is not a real concentration-point for the theoretical act of thought.

Kant himself did not raise this problem because the dogma concerning the autonomy of theoretical thought forced him to eliminate the entire transcendental complex of problems from the theoretical attitude. He believed that one can point to a *subjective* pole of thought, within the logical aspect, the *cogito* (I think), which is set over against all empirical reality as its necessary correlate of consciousness, and that this subjective pole has to be considered the transcendental logical point of reference for all the synthesizing activity of understanding (including both the so-called *a priori* and the empirical activities). Kant says that the "I think" must be able to accompany all my representations in order for them (in all their theoretical diversity) to be *my* representations. It is a final subjective logical unity of the experiencing consciousness which no longer, according to Kant, includes a multiplicity of moments which would themselves require a synthesis. Hence it is an utterly simple unity which can never itself become an object (Gegenstand) of knowledge, because every theoretical cognitive act has to proceed from this "I think." It is a transcendental thinking subject which Kant also calls the "transcendental logical self," and that has to be viewed as a transcendental pre-supposition of every theoretical synthesis. Kant distinguished it sharply from what he calls the "empirical individual ego in space and time." As transcendental logical ego it is devoid of all individuality.

Kant also denies that we can draw essential self-knowledge from this transcendental logical concept of the thinking self. For, according to his epistemological view, human knowledge can only relate to the given

18

sense perceptions which are gained within the *a priori* forms of intuition of space and time, and are ordered, by means of transcendental logical categories of thought, into an objective empirical reality.

Has Kant succeeded in showing an immanent starting point (intrinsic to theoretical thought itself) which meets the demands posed by a genuinely transcendental critique of thought? The answer has to be an emphatic "no." Kant's "transcendental logical self" cannot possibly be a unified center of consciousness *above* the modal diversity of the horizon of our experience. It encompasses the unsolved problem of the relation between the thinking ego and its logical function of thought, and already as such it can never be a "simple" unity without multiplicity. The metaphysical conception of the *anima rationalis* (the rational soul) as simple substance, a conception Kant rejected in his *Critique of Pure Reason* as empty speculation, is here simply transposed by him into a "transcendental logical unity of apperception" which is equally rooted in mystification.

There is not a single "simple unity" to be found in the logical sphere, taken in its transcendental sense. Kant's transcendental subject of thought remains caught in the *logical* pole of the Gegenstand relation, which according to Kant's own theoretical premise has its counter-pole in sensibility, to which it necessarily corresponds. How then, in Kant's own epistemology, can the synthesis between the transcendental logical category and the material of sense experience in space and time proceed from the logical pole of thought? If the logical aspect of thought and the aspect of sense perception cannot be traced back to one another, as he himself emphatically states, then neither can the starting point for the synthesis be found in the former. By accepting as axiomatic that the synthesis proceeds from the transcendental logical subject of thought and is executed in the transcendental faculty of imagination, Kant has left the critical path of research and swept aside the real problem of the process of theoretical synthesis. As a result, the true starting point of his critique of knowledge has remained hidden.

Now, if no starting point for the inter-modal synthesis can be found in theoretical thought as such, then the concentric direction of this thought which is necessary for critical self-reflection cannot be of a theoretical nature either. It must be rooted in the selfhood as the individual center of human existence. This means that it is not possible to get through to the true starting point of theoretical thought without having arrived at genuine self-*knowledge*. At least it is not possible without having learned to know the real nature of selfhood as the supra-modal center of existence. So the starting point is no longer the so-called structural unity of the theoretical act of thought, for such a structural unity, which remains enclosed within the temporal horizon, can never be more than a unity in the diversity of the modal aspects of time, i.e. an *inter-modal* but not *supra-modal* unity. Such an inter-modal unity is no more than a temporal structure which as such cannot possess a central point of reference for all its modal aspects. For that reason the qualification of selfhood as an "act-center" remains a mystification as long as this center continues to be sought within the temporal act-sphere itself. If anyone believed he could find the center of existence in a "historical temporality" in an anticipatory direction, disassociated from all that is a "given" of experience, he would be forgetting that such a temporality can only be a theoretical abstraction from the integral horizon of time, which also embraces the givens and can only be identified with it by way of an absolutization. Nowhere does universal time as such offer a central point of reference in the sense of a *root-unity* of human existence, one that genuinely *transcends* the modal coherence of temporal aspects. Yet, every absolutization we can uncover in immanence philosophy implies such a radical reference point in terms of which the absolutization is executed.

It is proof of a lack of self-knowledge when people suppose they can secure access to the *root*-unity of human existence through an autonomous theoretical metaphysics. The traditional metaphysical concept of *being*, ignoring now its speculative origins, is an *analogical* concept which remains caught up in the cosmic spectrum of meaning-diversity and cannot as such be a concentration point for the theoretical act of thought. And the metaphysical concept of substance which is rooted in this notion of being is not able to give theoretical thought a concentric direction either, since it remains in a state of dispersion in the diversity of the substances adopted. The notion of the substantial simplicity of the rational soul (*anima rationalis*) adopted by Thomas Aquinas continues to be burdened by inner contradiction since the concept of rational soul is only the product of a theoretical abstraction in which there is no space for an absolute unity.

Now, the concentration of theoretical thought (itself caught up in the temporal diversity of the modal aspects) upon the self (as the root-unity both of our horizon of experience and of our temporal existence) is possible only in a simultaneous concentration upon the real or supposed origin of all that is relative. As long as we try theoretically to grasp the selfhood in itself as a self-enclosed "independence," it dissolves into nothing – in the utter negation of all definitions. For the self as the root-unity of our existence does not exist in itself. It truly transcends all conceptual understanding. It does indeed possess an existent nature, but not in the sense of an anticipatory historical temporality of human existence that is opposed to "givens." Rather, this existence has the radical biblical sense of a transcending creaturely image of the absolute origin, namely God, an image which constantly has to reach beyond itself to find both itself and its Origin.

In other words, the selfhood is the religious center of human existence which does in fact transcend the modal diversity of the temporal horizon, because by nature it concentrates all that is relative upon the absolute. The utterly central religious domain of consciousness may therefore in no way be confused with one of the modal aspects of the temporal horizon, *not* with the emotional-psychical, *nor* with the logical, *nor* with the moral, *nor* even with the faith aspect.

This last aspect, that of faith, is the temporal limiting aspect of this horizon, through which the religious tendency of our selfhood imparts itself to all the modal functions of our experience. But in terms of its modal structure it remains the faith aspect caught up in the modal diversity and the unbreakable inter-modal temporal coherence of aspects; it cannot be the root-unity of all the modal functions. Faith itself requires the supra-modal point of reference of consciousness which can only be found in the selfhood. It is I who believe, as it is I who think logically, feel, live, etc. Self-knowledge never occurs in the divergent direction of the temporal diversity of our existence, rather only in the concentric direction, in which the self becomes conscious of the dependency of all that is relative and seeks the expression of the unity of origin in its radical created unity.

This means that self-knowledge is dependent on the knowledge of God. Both take shape in the central grip of the absolute, upon the religious center of our existence, not in a supposed autonomous concept which arises from the activity of theoretical thought. Because we are in the grip of the absolute, we learn to know it as an encounter which is at the same time a *realization*. This knowledge does not occur outside our temporal cognitive functions; it permeates them and gives them a concentric direction. Nevertheless, this knowledge also transcends the temporal horizon of our experience with its modal diversity of aspects. It is central, not functional.

The fall into sin has turned this self-knowledge and knowledge of God into an apostate direction and obscured the image of God in the mirror of the self. But the religious nature of the center, or the heart, of human existence has not been lost as a result. Instead, the innate drive of the selfhood to seek its origin now asserts itself in the absolutization of that which is relative, of something in creation. Humankind searches for itself and its origin within the horizon of time.

The darkened mirror of the root (*radix*) of our existence transforms the divine image into idols, false gods, to which the self *surrenders* in an imagined encounter in which it believes it can find *rest*. Even those who believe in all sincerity that they have broken with all religion and have no need for it continue to be in the grip of those idols, to which they devote all their energies. Human selfhood by nature points beyond itself.

This also implies that the selfhood, although it is in fact the individual root-unity of the consciousness to which the acts of theoretical thought are necessarily related, still cannot offer within itself the sought-after, deepest starting point of theoretical thought. The "I" is not self-enclosed like a windowless monad. It is only an "I" in the central communal relation of the "we" and in its existent relation to the "Thou" of its divine origin. In the "we," the "I" also steps outside of itself, in order to find itself and its origin in the existence of the human-rooted community. This root-community is of a spiritual kind, in the pregnant religious sense of the word, and is only made effective by a community spirit which as the central dynamic driving force gives human existence its final direction in its *religious ground-motive*. Philosophical thought which operates within the temporal horizon is no exception. It, too, receives its central direction from this source. Where the "I" is the hidden player on the instrument of theoretical thought, the central motif of the music proceeds from the community spirit operative in the individual centers of human existence. It is the religious ground-motive which determines the sought-after central starting point for the theoretical synthesis.

Here the transcendental critique of thought has hit upon the necessary *inner connection* between religion and philosophy. Since philosophy (through its theoretical total view of the horizon of experience and the empirical reality enclosed within it) gives to science in the narrow sense its necessary presuppositions, we have also penetrated to the inner connection between religion and science. From the inner structure and nature of the theoretical attitude itself, this root-penetrating critique of thought has brought to light the non-self-sufficiency of theoretical thought, i.e., that it is necessarily determined by the central and supratheoretical *dynamis* of the religious ground-motive. If for the sake of the dogma of autonomy it were to refuse to account for these supra-theoretical presuppositions of philosophical thought, it would cease to be critical and lapse into the theoretical dogmatism which *conceals* its true starting point. It does not help to try to escape from the transcendental critique of thought by appealing to the universally valid structure of human experience and theoretical thought. That *structure* is the same for all human beings but it does call for a central point of reference in the activity of theoretical thought, without which the structure cannot be *actualized* and which it cannot provide by itself.

Meanwhile, even the transcendental critique necessarily finds itself in the grip of a particular central ground-motive that gives direction to its own theoretical research. As long as it limited itself to the formulation of the transcendental problems forced upon it by the intentional structure of the theoretical attitude itself, it could have the appearance of proceeding from the same immanence standpoint whose illusory character it had just brought to light.

Such a situation may be observed, for example, in the work of Maurice Blondel. He consciously accepted the immanence standpoint as starting point for the purpose of demonstrating its non-self-sufficiency by the method of radically thinking through the implications of the intrinsic totality tendencies of philosophical reflection. Still, this neo-scholastic method cannot possibly lead to a genuine transcendental critique of thought. One who takes this road will not catch sight of the real transcendental problems of the theoretical attitude, because that person is dogmatically proceeding from the possibility of a theoretical autonomy of thought.

The philosophy of the cosmonomic idea does appeal to universally valid states of affairs when it conducts an investigation into the intentional structure of the theoretical attitude; at the same time, it makes clear that these states of affairs necessarily remain hidden from the theoretical view as long as the theoretical attitude of thought itself has not become a critical problem. For that reason, its posing of the transcendental problem is controlled from the start by those supra-theoretical presuppositions which are not exposed until the final stage of the transcendental critique.

Immanence philosophy, on the other hand, continues to conceal its necessary presuppositions behind the dogma of the autonomy of theoretical thought. And yet its formulation of the problems is also determined by a supra-theoretical and central starting point.

So the question becomes: which central starting point in fact makes possible the *radical* transcendental critique of thought itself? Which one frees the theoretical view from presuppositions which block insight into the integral horizon of human experience and its actual central point of reference? And which one at the same time reveals and explains such presuppositions in their true character so that the community of philosophical thought is not lost in the necessary confrontation of ground-motives?

## The Biblical Ground-Motive

The central starting point which meets these conditions is offered exclusively by the radical and integral ground-motive of the Word of God, that of creation, fall and redemption through Jesus Christ in the fellowship of the Holy Spirit.[1] This is indeed the "key of knowledge" because in the authentic Self-revelation of God it simultaneously discloses humankind to itself, lays bare the root-unity and root-community of its existence, and unveils the ground-motive of apostasy from God as the source of all absolutization. But precisely because it discloses the utter solidarity of the human race both in creation and in the fall into sin, it can never, as a starting point for philosophical thought, lead to a rupture of the community of philosophical thought. Rather, it puts *all* philosophical as well as theological reflection equally under its radical critique. This kind of transcendental critique of thought, which is really in the grip of this scriptural starting point, ultimately practices *self*-criticism when it expresses criticism of immanence philosophy, and it only continues this self-criticism by subjecting also the provisional and positive results of the philosophy of the cosmonomic idea to the critical process.

Having disclosed the necessary inner connection between philosophical theoretical thought and the central religious domain of human consciousness, the philosophy of the cosmonomic idea continues on its way by bringing into full view the religious ground-motives which controlled Western thought in its development from Greek antiquity.

The divergence of these ground-motives is only explicable in terms of the apostate direction in which the innate drive toward concentration of human existence begins to manifest itself, i.e. when humankind turns away from the Word of God from which alone it can draw spiritual life, and begins to search for itself and its origin within the temporal horizon with its intrinsic diversity of meaning.

---

1 This does not mean that the road towards a transcendental critique is closed to immanence philosophy. In that case the transcendental criticism would have broken the philosophical community of thought it actually sets out to serve. On the level of theoretic-philosophical reflection the philosophy of the cosmonomic idea constantly makes an appeal to universally valid structural states of affairs that would only remain hidden as long as the theoretical attitude of thought itself is not considered critically. That immanence philosophy by itself cannot manage to break through its own *dogmatic* standpoint does not demonstrate that it cannot, along the lines of our transcendental critique, be *brought* to a critical self-reflection upon its own central starting-point. It only precludes, in so far is its adherents consciously reject the biblical ground-motive, that they could ever come to *radical* self-knowledge revealing the apostate meaning of their central starting-point to them. The statement in the text merely wants to emphasize this point.

In the temporal horizon, the religiously unified meaning of the world that is concentrated in the human selfhood is broken up in a rich diversity of inseparable modalities and individuality structures. This horizon presents numerous possibilities for absolutization and for the formation of idols. The root of all divergence in ground-motives is the common spirit of apostasy itself. Its central driving power leads humankind away from its true origin and in its final consequence results in a meaningless *nothing*. To that extent the ground-motive of apostasy remains one and the same, regardless of the diversity in the modes of its manifestation.

The root of these apostate ground-motives is not eliminated by the central motive of divine Word-revelation, but rather is *unmasked* by it in its true character. For that reason this last-mentioned motive is not just one among several others but in fact the *only integral* and *radical* ground-motive which leads us to genuine knowledge of God and of self and also enables us to *really* know the human being and the world concentrated in that human being in its state of apostasy.

As such the biblical motive cannot lead to divergence in the starting point of Christian philosophy. When in Christian philosophical thought such divergencies in starting point nevertheless make their appearance, they can only be explained by the fact that unbiblical ground-motives have cropped up in the process, motives which scholars attempted to adapt to the biblical one. In this process, the biblical motive had to be accommodated to such an extent that it lost its radical and integral grip on human thought. Because such religious syntheses sought justification in orthodox or non-orthodox theological scholarship, the transcendental critique of thought has to remind people over and over again that the key of knowledge is not to be found in theological scholarship.

The unbiblical ground-motives of Western philosophy reveal their true character also in their theological synthesis with the biblical creation motive, through their inner dialectic structure. In fact, they consist of two central motives which are bound up in irreconcilable religious conflict and constantly drive philosophical thought that has come under their influence into opposite directions from one pole to the other. This religious dialectic is rooted in the absolutization of the relative, which only has meaning within time in unbreakable coherence of meaning with its own correlates. The absolutization breaks up this coherence in the illusion of an idol without being able actually to cancel it. Hence every absolutization of a *relatum* calls forth the corresponding *relata*. These correlata then emerge in religious consciousness as independent counter-forces against the dynamics of the first absolutized motive.

Since this conflict occurs in the central starting point of philosophical thought, it can never be resolved by a merely theoretical synthesis. Every theoretical synthesis demands a central point of reference which transcends the theoretical antithesis. But a conflict on the level of the ground-motive necessarily assumes an absolute character because there is no more basic starting point from which to launch a genuine synthesis. For that reason a *religious* synthesis cannot be brought about in reality; it remains an illusion. Only the biblical ground-motive shows the way to rise above the religious antithesis. This is not the way of a synthesis with the motive of the fall into sin, but that of real redemption from the power of sin through Jesus Christ who creates the fellowship of the Holy Spirit.

Since Greek antiquity, however, one still finds that attempts have been made in Western philosophy to resolve the radical antithesis in the ground-motive by means of a dialectic method of thought and so to establish a theoretical metaphysical synthesis. Such attempts are uncritical. The moment philosophical thought, caught up in the grip of a dialectic ground-motive, begins to undertake critical self-reflection, the metaphysical synthesis dissolves back into the ultimate antithesis of its starting point. As Proudhon wrote: "The antinomy does not resolve itself."

The religious dialectic of the ground-motive tends to drive philosophical thought, when it becomes self-critical, toward a dualistic picture of the human person and the world. In the process, the integral coherence of meaning of the temporal horizon of our experience is broken up into a dichotomy. This is also how the metaphysical oppositions between *noumenon* and *phenomenon*, immortal rational souls and material bodies, the "is" and the "ought," etc., arise. Periodically these oppositions are again thwarted by uncritical monistic conceptual tendencies.

Since a genuine resolution of the conflict in the dialectic ground-motive is not possible, there is only one critical mode of escape left. It is that of assigning primacy to one of the antithetic motives, a process that is inevitably accompanied by the devaluation of the other. The continual shift back and forth of primacy, the attempts at synthesis, and the critical dissolving of these syntheses back into the original radical antithesis are typical phenomena accompanying the influence of religious dialectic in the domain of philosophical thought.

## Western Dialectic Ground-Motives[1]

The philosophy of the cosmonomic idea has, through its transcendental critique of immanence philosophy, made an extensive study of the proc-

---

1   *Editorial note* (DFMS): Bos questions the *way* in which Dooyeweerd accounted for the *genesis* of the *unbridgeable dialectic tension* present in Greek thought (cf. Bos, A.P.: Dooyeweerd en de wijsbegeerte van de oudheid, in: Herman Dooyeweerd 1894-1977, Breedte en actualiteit van zijn filosofie, edited by H.G. Geertsema, J. Zwart, J. de Bruin, J. van der Hoeven & A. Soeteman, Kok, Kampen 1994,

ess in which Western philosophical thought has been caught up under the influence of these dialectical ground-motives. These ground-motives are: (1) the form-matter motive of Greek philosophy which permeates all of Greek thought at its roots and governs even its conception of mathematics; (2) the Scholastic ground-motive of nature and supernatural grace which, through its attempt to unite the biblical motive of creation with that of the Greek form-matter motive (and in modern times with that of the Humanistic ground-motive), involves Christian thought in a dialectical process and lays the foundation for the modern secularization of philosophy; and (3) the Humanistic ground-motive of nature and freedom which completes this secularization and has led, in the most recent dialectic phase of immanence philosophy, to the fundamental crisis of a state of spiritually uprooted thinking.

## The Form-Matter Motive

The first ground-motive, which before Aristotle had no fixed name, originated in the conflict between the younger cultural religion of the Olympic gods and the natural religions of Greek antiquity. However little we know of the very divergent cultic forms of the latter, we do know that the theme of life and death was central. And it was specifically the Dionysian cult, imported from Thrace, in which this theme found full expression. In this cult the deity was not represented in any fixed form or figure. It was rather the vital current eternally flowing from the womb of mother earth; this vital current was venerated as a formless but material and divine principle of origin. Out of this divine ancient principle arose generations of mortal beings who sought to be embodied in a fixed form and were on this account subjected to the wrath of *Anangkē*, the terrifying and unavoidable fate of death. The form is not divine and cannot endure. In the ecstatic cult of Dionysus this was symbolized by the tearing up of an animal whose flesh was eaten raw. On approaching the god Dionysus, ecstasy led to an intrinsic break with the limitations of the bodily form to the point of immersion in the stream of divine life.

The religious ground-motive of this vitality cult, that of the divinity of the vital current and that of *Anangkē* as the avenger of every attempt to bind the vital current to any physical form, exerted a permanent and central influence on Greek thought and art. This is the original Greek motive of matter which had as its dialectic counterpart the motive of form implicit in the younger cultural religion of the Olympic deities.

---

pp.197-227. According to Bos however, the value of Dooyeweerd's analysis of this *dialectic tension*, remains fully in tact: "Naar onze mening blijft de waarde daarvan overeind" – p.220.

The latter was the religion of form, measure, and harmony. The Olympic gods left mother earth behind with its never-ending cycle of beginning and ending, of life and death. They were immortal. As deified forces of culture they took on personal form which invisibly shared in the quality of imperishability. But these supra-mundane deities had no power over *Anangkē*, which ruled over the earthly cycle of life and death. For that reason the Greeks clung to the ancient nature cults in their private lives while Olympic religion became merely the official religion of the Greek *polis*.

The Orphic cult was a movement of religious reform aimed at a religious synthesis between the Dionysian cult of the vital current and the Olympian cultural religion (the form motive of the latter was diverted, however, in the direction of the Uranian motif of the divine measure and harmony of the starry heavens). It is in this cult that the form-matter motive finds its first anthropological expression in a dualistic view of a person. The immortal rational soul, which originated in the astral heavens, fell down on the dark earth; on earth it was enclosed in the dungeon of a material body, and thus caught up in the cycle of origination, demise, and reincarnation. The cycle continued until by an ascetic lifestyle it had purified itself of the defilement of the earthly body and could again return to its heavenly home.

This form-matter motive, born of conflict between the antagonistic religions, was not, as a dialectic religious ground-motive, bound to the mythological and ritual forms of popular faith. Over against this faith Greek philosophy claimed its autonomy. But the religious ground-motive of form and matter continued to be its common starting point and determined the entire course of its dialectical development. It controlled its view of nature (*physis*), its metaphysical doctrine of being, its anthropology, its ethics and philosophical theology, as well as its view of the state and human society.

Its dialectical process ran from according primacy to the motive of matter by the Ionian philosophy of nature and Heraclitus' philosophy of life, to giving primacy to the motive of form in cultural religion. In the process, the material principle was reduced to the status of the principle of imperfection, and the divine *nous* as pure form was understood as being divorced from all matter.

From the uncritically held monistic conception of the origin (*archē*) of nature (*physis*), Greek thought is then driven, by way of Parmenides' rigid theory of being, toward the acceptance of two mutually irreducible principles of origin. Attempts at synthesis by means of a dialectic logic then lead to an analogical, metaphysical doctrine of being, which is given its first foundation in Plato's Eleatic dialogues and elaborated in his own way by Aristotle in his metaphysics. Matter, as being in potentiality, is related to the form of being as the goal toward whose actualization the natural process of becoming strives (*genesis eis ousian* in Plato's *Philebus*, the essential form as entelechy of the natural process of becoming in Aristotle).

But the analogical concept of being that was intended dialectically to unite the principles of matter and form, lacked a central starting point for this synthesis, and therefore, upon critical self-reflection, had to dissolve itself again in the absolute antithesis of the religious ground-motive. In Plato's *Timaeus* this final antithesis again comes to clear expression in the polar opposition between the form-giving activity of the divine *Demiurge* and the deviant cause of self-willed *Anangkē*; in Aristotle's *Metaphysics* it comes out in the polar opposition between pure matter and the pure actualized divine form.

**The Nature-Grace Motive**

The scholastic ground-motive of nature and supernatural grace originates from the attempt to accommodate the Greek form-matter motive and the radical biblical ground-motive to each other. In the scholastic theology of Thomism it gains its hold on Christian thought; it permeates Roman Catholic church doctrine, theology, philosophy and sociology. Reformed Protestant thought also, by and large, continues to be open to the religious influence of the scholastic ground-motive – as a result it soon loses its reforming impulse.

The Greek form-matter motive fundamentally excluded the biblical motive of creation. The scholastic accommodation of the Aristotelian view of nature to the church doctrine of creation led to a distinction between a natural and a supernatural sphere, the first being considered a relatively autonomous substructure of the second. The church doctrine held that during creation, a supernatural gift of grace was bestowed on human nature, viewed as being composed of an immortal, rational soul as its substantial form and a perishable material body. This supernatural bestowal was lost at the time of the fall, a loss which did not corrupt nature as such.

In this system there was no longer any room for the radical religious unity of human existence. As a result the creation motive, now accommodated to the Aristotelian view of nature, lost its radical grip on philosophical and theological thought. Nor was there any room left, at least in officially approved Roman Catholic scholasticism, for the radical nature of the fall and redemption of a person. In the meantime, Protestant scholasticism, which also accepted the Aristotelian scholastic view of human nature, came into conflict with that view by retaining the biblical standpoint regarding human nature.

In Thomistic scholasticism, the accommodated Aristotelian metaphysics, with its analogical doctrine of being and its culmination in a natural theology, became the relatively autonomous anticipatory stage of the church's doctrine of supernatural grace. The idea that nature has its primary cause in God as the unmoved Mover, together with the Aristotelian proofs for the existence of God, were proclaimed to be a natural truth to be grasped by the natural light of reason. This unmoved Mover was equated with the divine Creator, although the Aristotelian form-matter motive was intrinsically inconsistent with the notion of the "first Cause" as "creating Cause."

The synthetic conception of Thomas Aquinas assumed, and proceeded from, a natural harmony between the natural light of reason and the supernatural truths of the church. The inner connection between the two was located in the natural desire of reason for its supernatural perfection. The autonomy ascribed to natural reason was understood in a scholastic synthetic sense: viz., that reason, because it can only penetrate the truths of nature, can never conflict with the truth of revelation; and that philosophy has a serving function in relation to the theology of revelation. Implicit in this conception, naturally, is the scholastic accommodation of Aristotelian philosophy to church dogma.

But the inner dialectic of the nature-grace motive led, in the 14th century, to the dissolution of the Thomistic synthesis into a polar antithesis. The powerful nominalistic movement of later scholasticism, led by William of Occam, denied every link between natural and supernatural knowledge; nature and grace took separate paths. Natural intellect was denied every capacity to know things metaphysical, and natural theology was rejected along with metaphysics. The realistic criterion of truth made way for a nominalistic one.

Occam still assigned primacy to the sphere of grace. For him this implied the belittling of natural reason, which therefore had no value whatsoever as a preparatory stage for supernatural knowledge. But toward the end of the Middle Ages there emerged clear symptoms of a relocation of primacy in the sphere of nature. The first indication of this shift occurred in the secularization of the theory concerning the church in nominalistic scholasticism, a development which can already be observed in the work of Marsilius of Padua. In this way the nominalistic movement became the forerunner of Humanism.

## The Nature-Freedom Motive

The humanistic ground-motive of nature and freedom implies a complete break with the Christian scholastic motive of supernatural grace. It originates in a Copernican reversal of the biblical image of a person, a radical shift which takes us directly to a religion of human personality in which the entire biblical ground-motive is humanized. The movement of the Italian Renaissance is in fact energized and directed by the religious motive of a *renascimento*, in which one is reborn to be an utterly autonomous and free personality who remodels one's idea of God and nature in one's own image. This humanistic ideal of personality spreads from Italy to the other countries of Europe. The new motive of freedom, in which the biblical motive of redemption and human rebirth is secularized, also incorporates from the outset the creation motive in a humanized sense.

The divine Creator now becomes the deified reflection of the creative impulse which the new freedom motive calls forth in a human being. When Leibniz then calls the divine Creator "the great Geometer," this idea of God is merely the deified reflection of the human intellect which created the infinitesimal calculus. This requires an idol of a creative intellect which can carry the mathematical analysis of the cosmos through right into the contingent sphere of phenomena.

The humanistic motive of freedom evokes the new image of macrocosmic nature, which becomes a second "idol" and gains mastery over the modern person. The "discovery of nature" in the Renaissance period signals a new religious attitude toward the cosmos surrounding an individual within the temporal horizon. Modern individuals have emancipated themselves from all faith in authority and want, in total autonomy, to take their destiny into their own hands. They seek in nature an endless field for their own drive to expand and regard it with the limitless optimism of this new vision for the future. Nature, as the macrocosmic reflection of the new ideal of the religious personality, is deified. "Deus Sive Natura" turns into a religious motive which is merely the correlate of the humanistic motive of freedom, and therefore fundamentally different from the deification of *physis* (nature). The latter is found in Ionic natural philosophy under the primacy of the motive of matter.

Meanwhile, both in the freedom motive and in its correlate, the new motive of nature, there lurks a basic multiplicity of meanings, one that harbors many different tendencies. Born of a secularization of the biblical ground-motive, the humanistic ideal of freedom lacks the depth-character peculiar to Christian freedom, which touches the *root-unity* of human existence. Although modern autonomous humanity has been in religious contact with the Word of God which discloses the root of its existence, it again seeks itself within the temporal horizon and concentrates its religious impulses upon the temporal diversity of meaning of its existence. Autonomous humanity can seek its religious center in its moral, aesthetic or emotive function, but it can also seek it in autonomous scientific thought. The same multiplicity of meanings is present in the humanistic motive of nature.

Nature in its immensity, which since the Copernican revolution in the astronomical world image seemed closely tied in with the religious revolution of the image of a human being, could be regarded as a macrocosmic reflection of a person's creative aesthetic freedom. In that case, "Nature" is viewed as the creator of ever new forms of beauty and centers of free individuality. At that juncture, the modern individual is not yet aware of any dialectical tension in the ground-motive of nature and freedom. This is the still predominant aesthetic feature in the Renaissance's glorification of nature which recurs in Giordano Bruno's philosophy of nature. But nature can also be viewed in terms of the Faustian motive of mastery which permeated the humanistic ideal of personality from the beginning. In this case, autonomous science regards nature only as a gigantic object of domination, and the nature motive becomes the power motive of the modern autonomous individual. And it is this power motive which soon gains the upper hand.

Galileo and Newton laid the foundations for a mathematical physics, which in fact showed the way toward scientific mastery of natural phenomena in their mathematical and physical aspects. As soon as they did this, the new philosophy, driven by the humanistic ground-motive, thrust itself with religious dedication upon the new scientific method and elevated it to a universal model for thought, as the foundation of the entire philosophical view of reality.

The classic humanistic science ideal demanded a deterministic image of the world which, as a closed system of causalities, completely corresponded to its motive of domination. The methodological breakdown of all given structures of reality served this purpose. Hobbes, in the preface to his *De Corpore*, demanded this methodical destruction in the name of the *creative* task of logical mathematical thought.

But now the dialectical tension inherent in the humanistic ground-motive also becomes manifest. In the deterministic picture of nature, itself called forth by the humanistic motive of freedom, there is no room anymore for a free, autonomous individual. Nature and freedom become each other's adversaries. From this point on, humanistic thought is caught up in a restless dialectical process.

The dethroning of the mathematical science ideal and Rousseau's shifting of primacy to the motive of freedom takes place in the same Enlightenment period in which Hume's psychologistic critique of knowledge undermined the foundations of modern mathematics and physics, as well as the new metaphysics based on them. In Kant's critique of knowledge, humanistic thought enters the phase of critical self-reflection. Nature and freedom are now sharply separated with the aid of the old metaphysical contrast between *phenomenon* and *noumenon*.[1] Primacy is ascribed to the motive of freedom operative in practical reason. Nature is degraded to the level of a world of phenomena of the senses as constituted by the transcendental consciousness. Kant even refused to ascribe a divine origin to it. His idea of God becomes moralistic. God is a "postulate of practical reason" and the true core of the free personality is sought in the moral "pure will."

The science ideal can no longer threaten the autonomous freedom of the will since, with the aid of the form-matter scheme (transformed in a humanistic sense), this ideal is now restricted to the realm of sensible nature; freedom, as belonging to the supra-sensible realm of the "ought to be," becomes a matter of practical faith in reason. Thus Kant's separation of faith and science proves to be governed by the religious dialectic of the humanistic ground-motive.

The Restoration period ushers in the dialectical conversion of Kant's still rationalistic and individualistic concept of freedom into an irrationalistic and universalistic one. It turns from the rationalistic absolutization of law, the general rule, to the absolutization of subjective individuality and the unrepeatable "one-time" event in history.

The historical way of thinking now arises. Born of the irrationalistic and universalistic conversion of the freedom motive, it is elevated to the status of a new universal model for thought which leads to a historical view of reality. Simultaneously, an attempt is begun to give up Kant's critical separation of nature and freedom by means of a dialectic logic and to think of nature and freedom as dialectically unified in a higher synthesis (Fichte, Schelling, and Hegel). Turning against this post-Kantian idealism of freedom, positivism (Comte, *cum suis*) assigns primacy back to the motive of the domination of nature, and regards the freedom of autonomous human nature as a natural consequence of scientific progress. The historical way of thinking is now rationalized and viewed as the highest plane of the natural scientific way of thinking. Darwinism naturalizes the historical way of thinking into an evolutionary one. Marxism transforms Hegel's dialectical idealism into dialectical historical materialism. Historicism, born of the irrationalistic conversion of the free-

---

1 *Editorial note* (DFMS): This metaphysical contrast is also known in the form of the opposition between *essence* and *appearance*.

dom motive, now distances itself from the post-Kantian idealism which had restrained it.

It becomes a new science ideal which develops in dialectical tension with the humanistic ideal of personality and proves to be a far more dangerous adversary of the freedom motive than the scientific model of thought of classical determinism. It leads to a universal relativism which, though still pictured by Wilhelm Dilthey as a last step to liberate the autonomous human being from dogmatic preconceptions, nevertheless begins to affect the religious foundations of humanistic thought itself. Nietzsche already saw nihilism on the horizon as the abyss in which Western thought, under the influence of historicism, threatened to plunge itself.

The emerging nihilism is also fostered by modern technocracy and its concomitant treatment of a person as part of the masses. This enslaves the free personality to the domination motive, which is detached from the central religious command of love and its relation to the root of human existence. During this process of spiritual uprooting of modern thought, overwhelmed by historicism, existentialism arises as a protest against the inner decline of the autonomous human personality. With its founder, Søren Kierkegaard, it was still completely caught up in the dialectical tension between his Christian faith and the isolated position of the autonomous individual suspended in time. The individual rebels against Hegel's dialectic because it makes him a puppet of the dialectic unfolding of the Idea.

But with Karl Jaspers, Martin Heidegger (in his famous work *Sein und Zeit*) and Jean Paul Sartre, existentialism is totally humanized and becomes a final escape from the process of depersonalizing modern Western personality, which is reduced to the impersonal "general human being" ["Men"]. It becomes an attempt, by way of philosophical self-reflection, to restore to the humanistic freedom motive a content which it was in danger of losing under the influence of radical historicism. The existentialistic freedom motive, in dialectic opposition to the "given" as the objective product of a completely devalued humanistic domination motive in science and technology, now directs itself to the existence of the ego, but in its individual historical "temporalization." However, with Heidegger and Sartre, this existential freedom has no other perspective than death and "nothingness." It is a transcending of "being" in the direction of "nothingness." And in Jaspers' "philosophical faith" the existential thinker admits his failure to grasp the transcendent which in time continually conceals itself in ciphers (*"Chiffren"*).

The allotted amount of space prevents a more extensive discussion of the central significance of these motives for Western thought other than the foregoing extremely limited diorama. However, one cannot warn often enough against the confusion, self-evident from the immanence standpoint, between these central ground-motives and the so-called philosophical themes which naturally can be found in great diversity within one and the same philosophical system, and which are not reducible to one simple philosophical theme. The coherence of the rich diversity of philosophical themes only becomes transparent in terms of the central ground-motive. The scholastic Christian side often objects strenuously to the transcendental critique of thought insofar as it proceeds from a central ground-motive in the Word revelation. People see in this an arbitrary selection from the great diversity of "truths of faith" revealed in Holy Scripture, and continue to hang onto the idea that philosophy can only draw its "Christian principles" from the Bible via theology.

A scholastic theology rightly feels threatened by a transcendental critique which exposes its dialectical ground-motive. But it may not ignore the inescapable question concerning the "key of knowledge" which theological exegesis cannot provide. The scholastic ground-motive of nature and the supernatural removes theological thought from the radical and integral grip of the Word of God, thereby excluding the focus on the *root* of human existence. This also explains why people are able to see the central motive of creation, fall and redemption only as an arbitrary selection of biblical "truths of faith."

The motive of nature and grace is *ex origine* a synthesis motive. It introduced a dialectical duality within Christian thought by alternately providing a religious point of entry for the Greek and modern Humanistic ground-motives. Yet people believed they could still hold on to their Christian standpoint.

**The Three Transcendental Ideas**

Finally, we must briefly consider how religious ground-motives intrinsically permeate philosophical thought and determine its formulation of problems.

This occurs by way of three transcendental theoretical ideas that lie at the basis of all philosophical thinking and make the typical philosophical view of totality possible. These ideas are directly related to the three fundamental transcendental problems which, as we saw, unavoidably arise from the intentional antithetic structure of the theoretical attitude.

In the first place, every philosophy presupposes an *idea of the mutual coherence and interrelation of the modalities of our horizon of experience, which are set apart in opposition to each other in the "Gegenstand relation."* This idea also determines the basic common denominator under which these modalities are brought in order to distinguish them theoretically from each other. Not even existentialist philosophy can escape such a transcendental idea, as shown by the fact that Heidegger, in his *Sein und Zeit*, expressly poses the problem of the common denominator when he tries to ontologically distinguish the "given" from historical "being." Such a distinction is only possible in the transcendental "Gegenstand" relation. He poses the problem of the common denominator before accounting for the great modal diversity of the temporal horizon of human experience. This is exclusively due to the dialectical ground-motive of his thinking. This ground-motive pre-eminently requires the polar opposition between the *necessity* of the "given" and the *ex-istent freedom* of human "being" [*Dasein*]. Nevertheless this onto-*logy* posits this antithesis on the basis of the theoretical logical function of thought. Even Heidegger, in his existentialistic phenomenology, is aware that the *ontic* is not identical with the onto-*logical*.

The question how one views the interrelation and coherence of the modal aspects of our experiential horizon is in fact dependent on the *starting point* from which the theoretical synthesis in its inter-modal character is carried out. Theoretical thought is concentrated upon this starting point by a second transcendental idea in which the deeper *root-unity* (or, in the case of a dualistic ground-motive, the two supposed antagonistic roots) of the separated modalities is (are) grasped. And this second transcendental idea is itself again dependent on a third, in which theoretical thought relates the theoretical diversity and the transcendental idea of its coherence to an ultimate Origin (in the case of a dialectical ground-motive, to two antagonistic principles of origin).

Thus all conceivable philosophy is founded in these three transcendental ideas which, in their indissoluble coherence, form an essential *tri-unity*. In the philosophy of the cosmonomic idea, this tri-unity is called the *transcendental ground idea* or *cosmonomic idea* as the theoretical expression of the *religious law of concentration* of human existence. A *philosophy* of the cosmonomic idea is possible only in the concentric direction of the transcendental critique of thought in which the necessary presuppositions of the philosophical theoretical attitude are to be explicitly accounted for.

*Dogmatic* immanence philosophy uses its cosmonomic idea *implicitly* without being conscious of the transcendental significance of the latter. The cosmonomic idea itself is a universally valid condition of philosophical thought, but the *content* given to it is dependent on the religious ground-motive which governs this thought.

Finally, what is the benefit of this transcendental critique of thought, here only briefly summarized, for the mutual exchange of ideas between the different schools of philosophy? The answer is that it makes genuine contact of thought possible between them, which – however paradoxical this may sound – is cut off at the root by the dogmatic standpoint of the autonomy of philosophical thought.

Polarly opposed trends of thought, which belong together in their ground-motive and yet repel each other, can meet with better mutual understanding once they become aware that their opposing points of view are rooted in the same central ground-motive. On the other hand, schools of thought which proceed from a different ground-motive can similarly begin to understand that each philosophical point of view must, in the first place, be judged in terms of its own starting point, and that fruitful philosophical dialogue can only begin when the transcendental problems of philosophical thought *as such* are critically accounted for.

On this basis the dialogue between the philosophy of the cosmonomic idea and neo-Thomistic philosophy has been carried on for a fairly lengthy period of time, something that has led to increasing mutual depth of insight. But every school of thought, without distinction, is a welcome partner in this critical discussion, which replaces dogmatic defensiveness with mutual critical self-reflection, and replaces the *hubris* of exclusivism with philosophical modesty born of insight into the *relativity* of all philosophical totality views. Only one who loses sight of the central point of reference and the Origin of this relativity can come up with the delusion that the transcendental critique of thought must lead to a philosophical *relativism*. The standpoint of the philosophy of the cosmonomic idea concerning the relativity of philosophy is briefly summarized over against all relativism in its following pronouncement:

> *"Meaning is the being of all that has been created;*
> *it is religiously rooted and is of divine Origin."*

# The Meaning of History[1]

AT THE OUTSET it is necessary to draw a fundamental distinction between the historical aspect of temporal reality and history in the sense of concrete events that function in reality. The historical aspect constitutes the *how*, i.e., the *modal character* of history. Concrete historical events indicate the *what* of history.

In naive, pre-theoretical experience we *explicitly* grasp history in the real structures of persons, things and events as *typical totalities*, and by contrast, only *implicitly* from the perspective of the historical aspect. These concrete structures span all the modal aspects of reality in principle and group them into a typical whole.

This explains why, in our naive experience, we identify history with *what happened*. However, we do not come here to a historicistic interpretation of reality, since implicitly we remain aware of the inner boundaries of the historical aspect in its relationship to the other aspects of reality. And we would never reduce all of reality to history. Neither would we seek to reduce it to a complex of sensory impressions in the way that they are ordered by the synthetic cognitive categories which we employ in the natural sciences.

On the other hand, in the theoretical or scientific attitude of thought the aspect of history cannot remain implicit, because now we are primarily concerned with the theoretical delimitation of the field of research of historical science.

The naive definition of "history" as "that which has happened" does not provide a criterion for history as a specific science. The science of history has a limited field of vision. It does not research the full empirical reality of what has happened, but only one of its modal aspects.

Up to the present time the various philosophical attempts undertaken to find the criterion for a theoretical delimitation of the historical field of vision have not led to a satisfactory result. These attempts include: the ontological criterion of "becoming" or "development," the methodological criterion of "*individualisierende Wertbeziehung*" (Engl. lit.: "individualizing value-relation"); the genetic criterion in contrast to the systematic point of view; or the idealistic criterion of value realization.

---

1  "*De Zin der Geschiedenis*" – from: *De Zin der Geschiedenis*, edited by J.D. Bierens de Haan et.al., Van Gorcum & Comp. N.V., Assen, 1942, pp.17-27. Translators: *K.C. and A.L. Sewell*; Editor: *Magnus Verbrugge*.

None successfully identifies the meaning of the historical mode as an aspect of reality.

The meaning of history is primarily determined by the modal structure of the historical aspect of reality. This structure is a foundational and constant modal framework. It is a precondition of concrete history in the ontological sense.

Therefore, before we proceed further we must engage in a serious theoretical analysis of the modal structure of this aspect.

### The modal structure of the historical aspect

In the theory of the law-spheres the philosophy of the cosmonomic idea has shown that the structure of every aspect of reality contains an original core meaning – the modal meaning-nucleus. We cannot reduce it further in our theory. We call this the original modal meaning-nucleus. It qualifies the whole aspect and guarantees its irreducibility in relation to the other aspects of reality (modal sphere sovereignty of the aspects).

At the same time, however, the philosophy of the cosmonomic idea has shown that the modal aspects have been arranged in a time-order characterized by a coherence of meaning. This mutual coherence of meaning cannot be broken and expresses itself in the structure of each of the modal aspects, everyone of which is qualified by its own particular meaning-nucleus. The time-order and meaning coherence under discussion make themselves evident in an interweaving of these modal structures: the original meaning-nucleus in each modal structure is of necessity related to other (non-original) modal elements of meaning. These non-original elements point back to the nuclei of earlier aspects and are called modal *analogies*. Each meaning-nucleus is also related to (non-original) modal elements of meaning which point forward to the nuclei of later aspects.[1] In the philosophy of the cosmonomic idea we call them modal *anticipations*. The only exceptions occur in the case of the boundary aspects of reality: those of number and faith. Their structure departs from that outlined above. The first, the aspect of number, can possess no modal analogies, while the last, the aspect of faith, can possess no modal anticipations.

---

1 *Editorial note* (DFMS): Dooyeweerd views *time* as an encompassing dimension of reality, guaranteeing an order of succession (earlier and later) between the different aspects. Initially he called references to modally earlier aspects *analogies* and references to modally later aspects *anticipations*. Eventually he simplified this distinction and used the term *analogy* to encompass both these "inter-modal moments of meaning coherence" – which implies that we have to distinguish between *retrocipatory analogies* and *anticipatory analogies* (cf. *A New Critique of Theoretical Thought*, Vol.II, 1955:75).

In this manner every modal aspect reflects the entire temporal order and meaning coherence of all the other aspects (modal sphere-universality). This explains the apparent cogency and persuasive strength of all *"-isms"* in philosophy, including the *"-ism"* of *historicism* which is so dominant in modern thought.

## The meaning-nucleus of history

When analyzing the modal meaning of history we are primarily concerned with finding the modal meaning-nucleus of history. In order to do this, the modal structures of the other aspects must be taken into account by an analytical method of confrontation. The meaning-nucleus of the historical aspect also appears in the form of anticipations in the structures of earlier aspects. Inevitably it also appears in the later aspects in the form of analogies.

In the circle of historians there is agreement that the science of history has to limit its area of research to cultural phenomena. Indeed, this cultural qualification provides a clue to the modal meaning-nucleus of history. However, contemporary philosophy of history has come under the influence of the humanistic ground motive in modern philosophy with its polarity between nature and freedom, between the scientific ideal and the personality ideal. It has levelled down this cultural qualification by incorporating in the term "culture" all those aspects of reality which do not fall within the field of research of the natural sciences.

In this inexact concept of culture the *meaning-nucleus* of the historical aspect remained hidden. It was wrongly understood in its *typical meaning* as an aspect of reality. Rather, this nucleus should be identified as *free formative control*.

That we have indeed discovered the modal meaning-nucleus of the historical aspect here can be ascertained by the method of confrontation we mentioned above.

In the logical aspect we first find it among the modal anticipations of *logical* qualification. We meet *control* over the *logical form* first in *opened* up *theoretical thinking*, which attains this formative control by its *systematic* character. Pre-theoretical thinking is not opened up yet: it still lacks all control over its logical form and is rigidly bound to the sensory impressions of the function of feeling. Logical formative control has no original historical character. Rather, it is governed by the peculiar principles of the logical law sphere wherein the logical aspect is bound. Therefore, it is not satisfactory to call the forms of logical thought "culture" as such.

An unbreakable connection exists between the meaning of this historical anticipation in the modal structure of logical thinking and the original meaning-nucleus of the historical aspect. In the first place in its logical formation *theoretical* thinking *has* a historical development. In its controlling character it stands under the *guidance and direction* of free formative control in its *original historical meaning*.

In the modal structure of the logical aspect the controlling formative element appears in a non-original meaning as an initially *opened up, anticipating* configuration or outline. In all the aspects of reality, which follow the historical aspect in cosmic time, this formative element is found to be qualified by the corresponding meaning nuclei, and is found amongst the modal *analogies*. Even in their yet closed (non-anticipating) structure the formative element is essential. There can be no language without linguistic forms, no law without *juridical genetic forms* (e.g. law, rule, regulations, verdicts, agreements etc. etc.). The same pertains to the primitive, as yet closed situations, wherein these aspects appear in reality.

When the peculiar structure of the modal aspects is ignored, the obvious temptation is to separate this *analogical* cultural element in the post-historical aspects from the latter's qualifying modal meaning-nuclei. In doing that its analogical character is disregarded.

This blurring of the boundaries of the modal aspect structures, however, necessarily takes its revenge in antinomies.

The theoretical antinomy is always a criterion of the violation of modal sphere sovereignty and therefore may not simply be considered as the necessary result of the limits of human cognition.

With the aid of the method of confronting, as amplified below, an analysis of the modal meaning-nucleus immediately enables us to locate the place which the historical aspect takes in the temporal order of the aspects. This aspect is strategically situated between the logical and linguistic aspects of reality, as a further analysis, that cannot be pursued here, would bring to light.

The determination of the proper location of the historical aspect is indispensable for a further investigation into the modal meaning structure of history.

### The normative character of the historical aspect

The fact that the historical aspect is founded directly in the logical aspect guarantees the normative character of the modal meaning of history. We understand this normative character in a specifically historical sense, and not in the moral sense, i.e., the laws which govern historical development are of a normative character; they are historical norms. Without a relation to these historical norms, such facts would lose their historical meaning. To recognize the normative meaning of history does not mean that we obliterate the boundaries between norm and fact. Instead, we merely recognize the undeniable modal pluriformity of normativity.

Those who deny the normative meaning of history must nevertheless recognize it, however unintentionally, as soon as they introduce into the historical aspect the normative contrast between *historical* and *reactionary* or *un-historical*.

One cannot possibly use the term "reactionary" in a pejorative sense unless it assumes a specific norm for historical development. In this context the application of ethical norms as criteria completely fails us.

The contrary *historical / un-historical* is a modal analogy of the logical principle of contradiction that constitutes a logical norm for thinking. Only those creatures who possess the ability to engage in reasonable discernment and who have an analytical awareness are capable of being subjects in the historical aspect.

Where the facts of nature function in history, the only role they can play is an objective one. They can only assume a historical meaning in the relationship with historical subjects. A correct insight into this modal subject-object relation within the historical aspect – and into the normative character of the modal meaning structure of history – becomes especially important for the determination of the modal meaning of the concept of *historical causality*. This may remain totally unrecognized if we eliminate its actual normative character. Historical causality is a modal analogy of causality in the original (scientific) meaning of the physical aspect. The subjective meaning of *historical causality* presupposes the *historical accountability* of persons who freely use their formative control. Similarly, juridical causality presupposes juridical accountability to accountable persons. This holds in so far as it is subjective causality of a human act and not an objective causality, e.g. the fatal effect of the bite of a rabid dog.

Historical accountability is a modal analogy of the logical principle of *sufficient ground*, which we can only apply to subjects with rational discernment. A natural-scientific causal series only exhibits a never-ending chain where all causal factors are of equal value, at least in principle (the equivalence principle).

Natural factors can merely have a dependent modal object function in the historical aspect. They can only give rise to *objective* causal contexts with a historical meaning. They are historically relevant solely insofar as they impinge on the cultural life of a person as subject. Only the human being is subjected to historical norms.

In this manner we may also analyze the other analogies in the modal meaning of history, each in their turn (historical *power* as the analogy of *psychical-feeling influence*, historical *development* as the analogy of *biotic development*, and cultural *area* as a *spatial* analogy, etc.).

All of the modal elements of historical meaning thus far investigated also reveal themselves in primitive, as yet closed, cultures. However, they receive a deeper meaning in the process of cultural development in which the historical aspect unfolds the latent modal anticipations.

## Closed and opened cultures

The criterion for distinguishing between closed and opened cultures is of fundamental importance for the science of history, because the science of history can only research and investigate those cultures which have entered this opening process, i.e., those that have been taken up into the mainstream of *world history*. The science of history leaves the cultural side of the development of primitive cultures that have remained *outside* world history to ethnology, which must follow an essentially different method.

This criterion is also, of necessity, of a normative historical character. The first mark of the closed condition of a culture is the scope of social restrictions imposed on the cultural interaction of the people. The primitive society is enclosed in undifferentiated social forms, which exhibit an undifferentiated power sphere in their culture. In all spheres of life the individual is subjected to this power sphere. He is only considered as a member of the primitive community and not as an individual person. Whoever does not belong to the primitive community is an enemy, an outsider (*hostis, exlex*).

Such a culture begins to unfold by differentiation, integration and individualization; a culture opens up its first modal anticipation by disclosing the meaning of the aspect of social intercourse. As the cultural sphere thereby loses its undifferentiated "closed" condition it enters the cultural traffic of world history. The demand for cultural traffic is necessarily latent in the norm for historical development implied in its modal meaning. According to this norm every form of cultural isolationism stands condemned.

Subsequently the culture also discloses its modal anticipation with respect to the meaning-nucleus of the linguistic aspect: i.e. symbolical signification. It is not until this stage that what is historically significant differentiates itself from that which is historically insignificant (cultural symbolism). This gives rise to the normative impulse to symbolically record history in chronicles, historical narrations, memorials, etc. In the much more congruent course of a primitive culture the muse of history does not find material for the chronicling of memorable episodes.

An important third normative anticipation is now disclosed by the culture in its modal structure, i.e., the economic one. As a consequence of this cultural differentiation, none of the differentiated spheres may assert an exclusive authority over the individual and the remaining cultural spheres, if a culture is to develop harmoniously. Every excessive expansion of the area of authority of any cultural sphere (be it that of science, art, state, church, trade, etc.), i.e., every violation of the norm of cultural economy, *of necessity* results in a disharmony in the process of cultural unfolding. At the same time this discloses the aesthetic anticipation of culture. The judgement of world history is passed on such a disharmonious cultural unfolding (juridical anticipation). This is because a harmonious cultural development presupposes a love of culture, an unrestrained passion for cultural formation, in which every cultural sphere can devote itself to its task according to its own character. In this *love* of culture the *moral* anticipation discloses itself in the meaning of history.

If one were to ask about the origins of cultural disharmony, it appears that every cultural unfolding is ultimately directed by a *belief* on the part of the leading cultural power. This takes its starting point from the religious, supra-temporal root of all world history, in which, according to the saying of Augustine, the struggle is fought between the *civitas Dei* and the *civitas terrena*. From the Christian standpoint the human race has fallen away in its religious root. In the final analysis the radical fall into sin, brings an inevitable disharmony in cultural unfolding. The community of humankind has turned away from its Creator in the religious center of its entire existence. As a result its cultural unfolding exhibits a religiously apostate direction. This reveals itself in the absolutizing – and therefore the overextension – of that which is temporal and creaturely. Against every violation of the norm of cultural economy the tribunal of world history eventually claims a concomitant retribution, which itself in turn assumes a role in the cultural unfolding. The central conserving power, however, remains that of Christian belief.

### Concluding observations

The connection between belief and history calls for the formulation of an idea of development that would relate world history to the transcendent religious root of creation. The faith function itself remains part of the temporal world-order, and may therefore not be confused with the transcendent religious core of temporal reality. The faith-function is the transcendental boundary function of temporal existence, which pertains to this distinctive law sphere.

The modal structure of belief or faith expresses the transcendental boundary position this final aspect occupies between time and eternity.

The modal meaning-nucleus of the function of faith is transcendental certainty in time concerning a transcendent firm ground and origin of that which is created and which reveals itself in time. Faith *points beyond time*.

In the structure of the faith aspect all modal analogies partake in this transcendental boundary character (e.g., the element of adoration inherent in all faith, which is an analogy of moral love; the juridical analogy concerning the right of God to be adored; the aesthetic analogy of the harmony between the finite and the infinite, the economic analogy of preparedness to sacrifice when considering temporal and eternal values; the social analogy of a relationship of faith with the absolute Origin of all things; the linguistic analogy of faith-symbolism, etc.). Faith is always related to a revelation of God in his works or in the nature of the creation. In its true meaning it is first explained in the Word-revelation.

By contrast, apostate faith interprets the revelation of God in the "nature of the creation" according to its own apostate fantasy (cf. mythology).

Every absolutization, including every one of those in philosophy, is ultimately an act of faith and can never be explained in purely theoretical terms. It is an act of faith because it proposes a sure ground for the thinking process, which can only be found in the Absolute.

There is a transcendental boundary point in all apostate faith, i.e., the apostasy of the deification of natural forces, which are not understood (mana religion). At this boundary point the pagan nature-bound faith keeps the whole culture under its control in a rigid and closed condition. It keeps its culture rigidly bound to its deified natural-substratum, and this renders any enfolding of the anticipatory cultural spheres impossible.

# The Criteria of Progressive and Reactionary Tendencies in History[1]

THE COMMEMORATION OF the 150th anniversary of the Royal Dutch Academy of Sciences and Humanities provides occasion for historical reflection. It will not be a matter for surprise, therefore, that in considering the question as to which general subject might be best suited to this commemoration I have chosen a fundamental problem of the philosophy of history, i.e., the problem, whether we can point to objective criteria that will make it possible to distinguish between progressive and reactionary tendencies in history.

In the conflict of politics the opposite terms "progressive" and "reactionary" are often used in a demagogic sense. In earlier days the liberal parties laid claim to the designation "progressive." Later on the socialist parties did the same. Nowadays the totalitarian parties demand the exclusive right to call themselves "progressive" in contrast to all the others that reject their ideology. Of course it stands to reason that these totalitarian parties would not accept being designated "reactionary." They, too, in general stress the progressive character of their political programmes, at least in so far as they have not abandoned the belief in progress in its politico-historical sense. The situation demonstrates that there can be different views of the so called demands of historical development. Yet it is without question that in both cases truly historical standards or norms of historical development are at issue. Can such standards have an objective basis in the inner nature of history itself, or are they nothing more than unverifiable measures of a merely subjective appreciation of the course of a historical process? It is to this question that I shall devote some observations this morning.

It will be evident that it is not only to the *politician*, who seeks from a study of the course of history to understand the demands of the present and the near future, that this question is important. The historical process

1 An address delivered to the *Koninglijke Akademie van Wetenschappen* (Royal Academy of Sciences and Humanities) in Amsterdam on the occasion of its 150th anniversary May, 1958, N.V. Noord-Hollandse Uitgeversmaatschappij, Amsterdam, pp.213-228. Translated by the *Academy*; Edited by *Magnus Verbrugge*.

moves in the historical aspect of time, in which past, present, and future are inseparably interwoven with one another.

The *historian*, whose scientific attention is directed to the past, is equally confronted with the problem as to whether objective criteria for a distinction between progressive and reactionary tendencies in history can be discovered. And here, too, this distinction is doubtless of a normative character, since the question at issue is whether norms of historical development of a verifiable validity do exist by which the factual course of historical events may be tested.

## The elimination of normative viewpoints from scientific historiography

For this very reason the well known neo-Kantian philosopher Heinrich Rickert, who has paid much attention to the epistemological foundations of cultural science as distinct from those of natural science, denied to the science of history any judgement concerning progressive and retrograde tendencies in the process of historical development. In his opinion such axiological judgments exceed the bounds of both the science and philosophy of history and should be reserved for personal world-and-life-views only.

The question whether such an elimination of all normative viewpoints from a scientific historiography and philosophy of history is possible may be left aside for the moment. Provisionally, it will be sufficient to establish that the normative contrast between progress and regress or reaction is closely connected with the fundamental notion of historical development.

There is hardly room for doubt that it is this very notion which enables the historian to discover inner coherences in the temporal succession of historical facts and changes. If this notion were to be eliminated, as, from a positivistic viewpoint, J.H. Kirchmann advocated in the nineteenth century, no synthetic insight into a process of history would be possible and historiography would degenerate into a collection of mixed reports from the past.

But the fundamental concept of development or evolution evinces the general condition of all basic concepts of the various academic disciplines: it is in itself of an analogical or multivocal character, with the result that it is also used in other disciplines, although in a different modal sense. In a lecture previously delivered in the section of humanities of this Academy I drew special attention to this remarkable fact. It appears to be rooted in the structure of the temporal horizon of human experience, and more precisely in that of the different fundamental modal aspects of this experiential horizon which in principle delimit the different viewpoints from which empirical reality may be approached by the different special branches of science. The historical aspect is only one of these fundamental modes of experience, which in themselves do not refer to the concrete *what*, that is, the concrete things or events of temporal reality, but rather to the modal *how*, i.e., the manner in which they are experienced in their different aspects.

These fundamental modal aspects of temporal human experience are arranged in an irreversible temporal order which expresses itself in the modal structure of each of them. This structure determines their modal meaning. In tracing this modal meaning we are confronted with a nuclear moment which guarantees the irreducible character of the aspect concerned. But the nucleus of this modal meaning can reveal itself only in an unbreakable coherence with other structural moments referring backwards or forwards respectively to all other modal aspects which are arranged either earlier or later in the temporal sequence. Since these other, non-nuclear, moments in the modal structure of an aspect give expression to the universal inter-modal coherence of the meaning of our experiential horizon, they are in themselves of an analogical or multivocal character. It is only the irreducible modal nucleus of the aspect in which they occur that can give them a univocal sense.

### History is not what has really happened in the past: historicism

If we are to apply this insight to the historical aspect of our experiential horizon, it must be established, firstly, that this mode of experience is not to be identified with *what has really happened in the past*. Concrete events, even those which in a typical sense are called "historical facts," function in principle in all experiential aspects. Their historical aspect can only be a particular *mode* of experiencing them. Secondly, it must be clear that in speaking of historical development we refer to an analogical moment of meaning whose modal sense is determined by the nuclear moment of this aspect. But what, then, is the modal nucleus of the historical mode of experience?

Here we are confronted with the fundamental question which is ignored as a matter of principle in the current epistemological views of the nature of scientific historiography. This is explained by the fact that in modern Western thought the historical mode of experience is no longer viewed as a specific modal aspect of empirical reality, but much rather as being identical with this reality, or at least with the empirical reality of human society. This view has found expression both in De Bonald's statement: *"La realité est dans l'histoire"* and in Von Ranke's conception of the task of scientific historiography as a description of *"wie es eigentlich gewesen ist."* It implies that all normative aspects of the life of human society, i.e. those of social interaction, language, economic administration of scarce goods, aesthetic appreciation, law, morality, and faith are historicized. In other words, we are confronted with a historicistic view of temporal reality, originating from an absolutization of the historical aspect of experience. In a similar way the absolutization of the physico-chemical aspect of energy, or of the biotic aspect, or the psychic aspect of emotional feeling and sensation gives rise to an energetistic, a vitalistic, or a psychologistic view of reality.

It should be realized that this historicistic view of the world was originally postulated as the view that in effect dialectically opposed the naturalistic picture of reality which issued from an overstretching of the mathematical natural scientific view-point of classical physics. Both these naturalistic and historicistic views of reality had their common origin in the Copernican revolution of philosophical thought initiated by Descartes. Both resulted from a methodical demolition of the given structural order of human experience based upon the divine order of creation. The modern idea of the autonomous freedom of human personality which involves both its thought and its activity was incompatible with the acceptance of any given structural order; for a given order of creation meant theonomy. The Cartesian turning to the subjective *cogito* as the ultimate ground of certainty was entirely in keeping with the religious basic motive of the form of Humanism which arose at the time of the Renaissance. It was rooted in the motive of nature and freedom, as it has been styled since Immanuel Kant.

As a secularization of the Christian conception of human liberty, the humanistic freedom motive was quite different from the classical Greek idea of the autonomy of human reason. It implied ascribing to the human mind a creative power to project a world after it's own image and to have complete control of its own future. It elevated the human personality to an absolute end in itself, which implied a radical reversal of the biblical view of the relation between God and the human ego created after God's image. It evoked also a new concept of nature as the macrocosmic counterpart of the emancipated human ego, which at the time of the Renaissance gave rise to a deification of nature *(Natura sive Deus).* The Faustian striving after a complete domination of nature required a strictly deterministic picture of natural reality envisaged as an uninterrupted chain of functional causal relations which could be formulated in mathematical equations. The new mathematical physics founded by Galileo and Newton provided the scientific methods whereby to reconstruct the world theoretically in keeping with this Faustian motive of domination.

But nature, as an objective reflection of this motive of domination, left no room for the freedom of human activity.

Thus the religious basic motive of nature and freedom displayed, as the ultimate hidden starting-point of modern Humanistic thought, a dialectical tension between two opposite motives. It involved modern philosophy in a dialectical process in which primacy was ascribed alternately to one of these competing motives, with the result that the effect of the other was depreciated.

Whereas under the primacy of the mathematical science-ideal Cartesian philosophy developed in an anti-historical direction, the Italian thinker G.B. Vico was the first to place his "new science" ("*nuovo scienze,*" the science of the history of humankind which in an unclear way he called "philology") in opposition to the mathematical pattern of thought. But this new science was not at all delimited with respect to its specific modal viewpoint in such a way that the absolutization of the historical aspect of our experiential horizon was avoided. It started, rather, from the humanistic motif of creative freedom of the autonomous human mind, which essentially seeks to break through the given structural bounds of the modal aspects of empirical reality. Vico's fundamental thesis is that our civil world is undoubtedly created by human beings in the process of history, so that its origins must be sought in the human mind. Thus the science of history is conceived as the science of the temporal genesis of humankind, which has created itself in the whole of its cultural existence and therefore knows itself from the whole inheritance of its culture, with the result that in this science subject and object are identical.

But the temporal genesis of humankind cannot be a specific scientific viewpoint, since in principle this genesis functions in all the modal aspects of our experiential horizon. It is a real process occurring in the full continuous coherence of time and not merely in a specific historical aspect of the latter. Therefore it is of no avail to say that the historical viewpoint is the genetic viewpoint, without indicating the modal sense of this latter. The physico-chemical or the biotic aspect of this genetic process is doubtless of no concern to historical research in its proper sense. Vico, in fact, did not include these aspects in the field of his new science. Starting from the basic motif of nature and freedom he established (with a particular emphasis directed against the Cartesian science-ideal) that nature has not been created by humans but by their culture. Consequently the history of humankind is restricted to the whole of humankind's cultural activity and its results. Since the time of Vico this has become the prevailing view; for the earlier restriction of historiography proper to political history, or even to that of wars and battles, is quite arbitrary and inadequate. On the other hand, it is meaningless to set the latter in opposition to cultural history since without human culture there can be neither peaceful political life nor human wars and battles.

But is culture to be viewed as a concrete, ever-changing temporal reality of a specific kind, or is it one irreducible modal aspect of temporal reality? According to Vico, it is the historical realization of eternal ideas in the social life of nations, the product of their collective mind or consciousness, the "civil world," as he calls it. It embraces their customs, their law, their language, their fine arts, their economic relations, their religion, their scientific life, their social institutions.

Here we are confronted with the source of modern historicism; for history in its proper sense is the history of human culture and culture itself is a historical reality embracing all the normative aspects of temporal human life. Hence all our norms and values and all our social institutions are nothing but the historical products of a specific cultural mind in a particular phase of its development.

This radical historicism is the dialectical opposite of the *a priori* humanistic doctrine of natural law developed, *more geometrico*,[1] under the primacy of the mathematical science-ideal. In Vico this opposition could not yet reveal itself as an exclusive alternative since his historicistic view of temporal human life was tempered by his belief in eternal ideas, which are realized in the history of humankind with the inner necessity of a divine Providence. It is the same Providence which, in his opinion, also guides the cyclical course of history in its progressive and regressive movements, its *"corsi"* and *"recorsi."* This means, with regard to the province of law in human society, that all positive law is nothing other than a positivization of the eternal principles of natural law, which in consequence are embodied in historical reality. This component of natural law is, according to him, the moment of rational truth in any legal order. The moment of cultural positivization is that of certitude and corresponds to the moment of power in history.

This latter view, that the cultural activity of humankind is an unfolding of power, is of extreme importance in Vico's theory, though it is explained by him only in passing; for it will be seen that it provides the clue to the solution of our previous question, namely: what is the nuclear moment of the historical mode of experience? A satisfactory answer to this question is tantamount to a fundamental overthrow of the historicistic world-view, though this is something which Vico himself could not achieve, since a historicistic view of temporal reality cannot be rendered harmless by a belief in eternal ideas. Supra-temporal ideas of justice, beauty, goodness, and so on, are nothing but a metaphysical absolutiza-

---

1   That is, in a geometric fashion – Translator.

tion of normative modal aspects of our temporal order of experience, whose differences of meaning can exist only in the order of time. For it is this order of time which breaks the radical religious unity of all meaning into a successive plurality of modes. Historicism has an inner tendency to emancipate itself from any belief in eternal ideas; for human belief is also included in the temporal horizon of consciousness and historicism identifies true time with historical time. If belief belongs to human culture, then the so called eternal ideas can only be the ideological component of a culture in a metaphysical phase of its historical development. Accordingly they can have only a historical significance.

Historicism in its consistent form means the historicizing of our entire temporal horizon of experience and of the central religious reference point of the experiential horizon, namely, the human I-ness in its relation to other egos and to the Divine Author of all creation.

The absolutization of the historical aspect begins with the elimination of its modal structure by which its general meaning is determined and restricted. This structure cannot be changeable in time, since it is the condition which alone makes the historical mode of experience possible. Consequently it cannot be identified with a variable historical phenomenon presenting itself in this experiential mode.

We are seeking the irreducible nuclear moment of this structure. The etymological derivation of the term "history" does not help us in our search. The word is of Greek origin and initially had the neutral sense of "investigation." The qualifying nuclear moment of the particular experiential mode which determines the viewpoint of historical science proper is much more likely to be discovered through an epistemological analysis of the concept of culture, because we have seen that the notions of becoming and of development, with the aid of which it was attempted to delimit this specific historical viewpoint, are in themselves multivocal. In the last instance, it is only the *cultural mode* of development that can give the analogical concept of development its historical sense. It is for this reason that all gnoseological investigations concerning the specific historical viewpoint were centered on the fundamental significance of the concept of culture for the historical mode of thought.

We have also seen that historicism viewed the whole of human society in all its normative aspects as an historico-cultural product. Consequently the absolutization of the historical aspect of experience must be closely connected with the absolutization of the concept of culture. The use of the noun "culture" may easily give rise to the erroneous opinion that here a particular kind of reality is meant, a concrete *"what."* Every absolutization of a specific experiential aspect begins by identifying this aspect with concrete reality, although the latter has in fact *many* modal functions. But a particular kind of reality, which is entirely cultural in character, cannot exist. Let us, therefore, replace the noun "culture" with the adjective "cultural" in order to emphasize that it is only a modal aspect of empirical reality that is meant. Taken in this modal sense, the term "cultural" means nothing more than a particular manner of formation which is fundamentally distinct from all modes of formation found in nature. It is a controlling mode, whereby form is given to a material in accordance with a freely elaborated project.

A spider spins its web with faultless precision; but it does so after a fixed and uniform pattern, prescribed by the instinct of the species. It lacks free control over the material with which it works. Conversely, the cultural mode of formation must receive its specific modal qualification through formative freedom, control, or power. This is why the great cultural commandment given to humankind after the creation of the world reads: "Subdue the earth and have dominion over it."[1] And if the genuine historical viewpoint of historiography is that of cultural development, it follows that formative power or control must also be the nuclear moment of the historical aspect which gives the analogical concept of development its proper historical sense.

The cultural mode of formation reveals itself in two directions which are closely connected with each other. On one hand, it is a formative power over persons unfolding itself by giving cultural form to their social existence; on the other hand, it appears as a controlling manner of shaping natural things or materials to cultural ends.

The Germans speak of *"Personkultur"* and *"Sachkultur."* Since all cultural phenomena are bound to human society in its historical aspect, the development of *Sachkultur* is in principle dependent on that of *Personkultur,* because *Sachkultur* can develop only in a historical subject-object relationship and only human beings in their social relations can function as subjects in the cultural process of history. In addition, both *Personkultur* and *Sachkultur* presuppose the leading ideas of a project which leading figures or groups in history seek to realize in a human community. It is for this reason that the formative power of these leading figures or groups always bears a relationship of intention to such ideas.

These ideas cannot be brought to fruition merely on the basis of the subjective conception of those who propagate them. They must assume a socio-cultural form so that they themselves may be able to exercise formative power in the relationships of society. By way of illustration I

---

1  Gen.1:28 reads: "And God blessed them, and God said unto them, be fruitful, and multiply, and replenish the earth, and subdue it: and have dominion over the fish of the sea, and over the fowl of the air, and over every living thing that moveth upon the earth."

might point to the cultural influence of the ideas of natural law and of the Roman *ius gentium,* or to the influence of the technical ideas of great inventors, or the aesthetic ideas of great artists, or the religious ideas of the preachers of a new belief. Such ideas are not of a cultural-historical character in themselves; but they acquire a historical significance as soon as they begin to exercise formative power in human society. They can be realized only in typical social structures of individuality which in principle function in all aspects of our experiential horizon. The empirical reality of human social life can, therefore, never be exhausted in its cultural-historical aspect. All that is real or that really happens in human society is more than merely historical.

**The concept of historical development**

Having established in this way the modal nuclear moment of the historical aspect of experience, we may now turn to the analogical concept of historical development. The question we asked was whether the normative contrast between progressive and reactionary tendencies in the process of historical development may be based upon the modal structure of the historical aspect of experience. To answer this question it is necessary to examine somewhat more fully the analogical moments of meaning of this structure.

The moment of development in history refers back beyond doubt to that kind of development which we find in the biotic aspect of experience. But it does not do so directly. The cultural-historical aspect is immediately founded in the logical aspect, that is, the aspect of analytical distinction. Rickert assumed that the historical mode of experience is constituted by a logical category of culture by means of which, in an individualizing manner, natural reality in space and time would be related to a supra-temporal realm of values. This cannot be right. Culture is not a logical mode of experience. Nonetheless, without the logical foundation of the analytical mode of distinction, there can be no historical mode of experience. And this connection between the logical and historical aspects finds expression, in the modal structure of the latter, in analogies of the fundamental logical relations of identity, diversity, implication, and contradiction. I shall merely point to the analogy of the logical relation of contradiction in the historical mode of experience. A logical contradiction takes place when an argument contains two contradictory propositions. Such reasoning is called illogical, in contrast to a logical sequence of thought. This contrast is of a normative character since an illogical argument violates a fundamental norm of logical thought.

Now it is indisputable that in all aspects of experience, which are founded in the logical aspect, an analogy of this normative logical contrast is found. This is a strong indication of the normative character of these contrasts, which means that, within these experiential modes, human behavior is not subject to laws of nature but to norms. I refer to the contrasts between polite and impolite, decent and indecent, and so on, which function in the aspect of human social interaction; to the contrast between linguistically right and wrong, which functions within the linguistic aspect; to the contrasts between aesthetic and unaesthetic, lawful and unlawful, moral and immoral, believing and unbelieving, which respectively function in the aesthetic, juridical, moral and certitudinal aspects of our experiential horizon.

The contrast, then, between progressive and reactionary movements in the process of historical development is clearly an analogy of the logical principle of contradiction. It must be founded in the inner structure of the historical aspect, since this aspect is also based upon the logical. If it makes sense to speak of the demands of historical development – and the only ones who refuse to do so are those who are prejudiced by the dogma that even the so called cultural sciences should refrain from any normative judgement – then the distinction between progressive and regressive tendencies cannot be the result of a merely subjective evaluation.

No one who thinks in truly historical terms will deny that from a politico-historical viewpoint the so called counter-revolutionary movement in the first half of the nineteenth century, which strove for a restoration of the medieval Germanic feudal regime with its undifferentiated patrimonial conception of political authority, was of a reactionary character. This judgment will be independent of the question whether or not the memory of those times is evoked with a certain romantic desire. But on what objective norm of historical development may this judgment be founded?

The German historical school of jurisprudence, whose philosophical conception of history was strongly influenced by Herder and Schelling, has laid particular stress on the organic character of any true historical development. Taking the natural development of a living organism as a pattern, von Savigny and his followers believed that every nation brought forth its culture from its own individual "national spirit" in a process of organic continuity, connecting the present and future with the past. But in the historical tradition of a people they distinguished both living and dead elements. The former are to be utilized in further development, but the latter should be sloughed off. As long as a national spirit was really productive, its culture, including its political and legal institutions, was the result of natural growth and not the artificial and mechanical product of a rationalistically minded epoch. It is evident that in this view the biotic analogy in historical development is strongly stressed.

Nevertheless, there can be no question here of a naturalistic misinterpretation of cultural evolution; for this is excluded by the fact that in its philosophical background this organic view of history originated in the post-Kantian German freedom-idealism.

In line with Schelling, von Savigny regarded history as a dialectical synthesis of autonomous freedom and natural necessity. The latter, however, was not envisaged as a mechanical causality governed by general laws. After Kant the humanistic basic motive of nature and freedom underwent an irrationalistic turn. The rationalistic conception eliminated all individuality from its world-view by reducing all individual phenomena to general laws. The irrationalistic conception, on the other hand, used as its starting-point the irreducible individuality of any real whole and denied its subjection to general rules. The historical school rejected the rationalistic natural-law view of human society with its general *a priori* patterns of law and state, which it thought to be applicable to any people and any age.

Every nation brings forth its own law and political constitution from the full individuality of its collective mind. It does so in autonomous freedom in the process of historical development and in an individual way. History lacks general laws. There is, nevertheless, a hidden law of providence (or *"Schicksal"* in a more pagan version) which directs this process in such a way that it also shows an inner natural necessity elevated above all human arbitrariness. This hidden law of historical process, already to be found in Fichte's philosophy of history, could not fail to assume an irrational normative sense. And it was the Lutheran legal philosopher and statesman Fr. Julius Stahl who openly accepted this consequence. In his opinion all that has come about in a long process of historical development, under the influence of incalculable and inscrutable forces, without the interference of rational human planning, ought to be respected as a manifestation of God's guidance in history, in so far as it does not contradict God's revealed commandments.

This conception of God's guidance in history was quite in line with the conservative mind of the *Restoration*. Apart from its romantic-quietistic formulation, it had a great influence on the so called Christian-historical theory of the nineteenth century. The latter accepted the new historical mode of thinking as a powerful ally in the conflict with the tenets of the French revolution.

Meanwhile this ascription of a normative sense to God's guidance in history was open to serious objections. These objections were amply set forth in a remarkable thesis defended in 1911 at the University of Leyden by A. C. Leendertz. From the theological viewpoint this author argued that God's guidance embraces all that happens, both good and evil.

For that reason this guidance pertains to God's hidden counsel and cannot imply any norm for human behavior. From the philosophical viewpoint Leendertz attacked the normative conception of God's guidance in history with the Kantian argument that empirical facts and norms belong to different worlds. If the factual course of history is elevated to a norm, then that is tantamount to a continuous acceptance of the *"fait accompli."* If a governing dynasty is supposed to be justified by the fact that it has maintained its power over a long period of time, then a revolution overthrowing that dynasty is also justified after a period of having successfully maintained its position.

This philosophical critique must fail inasmuch as it started from the Kantian separation between empirical facts and norms, which dualism is rooted in the dialectical humanistic motive of nature and freedom in its critical conception. It overlooked the consideration that historical facts are not given in the same way as natural events and that in the normative aspects of human experience no single fact can be established without making use of a norm. It could not do justice to the view of the historical school since the latter did not mean to elevate any solely factual course of events to the level of a historical norm. The concept of organic historical development cannot have a solely factual content apart from a normative criterion whereby to establish what is and what is not in keeping with it. Von Savigny's distinction between living and dead components in the historical tradition implied a rejection of any factual attempt to revive that which had lost its historical significance in the organic development of culture. It implied, in other words, a distinction between progressive and regressive movements in history. Thus it was manifested based on a normative criterion.

But what was this criterion? In the final analysis it was derived from the individuality of the national spirit, viewed as the true source of national culture and as a gift of Divine Providence having value in itself. It was supposed that organic continuity in cultural development was guaranteed only by the directive potency of the national spirit (*"Volksgeist"*) which operates in conformity with the hidden law of Providence. This irrationalistic view of the norm of historical evolution can lead to very dangerous consequences, especially if it is accompanied by a historicistic view of the norms of law, morality, and faith. The Nazi movement in Germany was only too ready to welcome these consequences, as was apparent from Hitler's assertion that Divine Providence had destined the German people to be a nation of rulers.

The subjective individuality of a national character can never be a cultural norm in itself. It will always show both good and bad traits, apart from the fact that it is very difficult to establish the characteristic traits of a particular nation as a whole. And even though it were considered a gift of God, it is certainly not left unaffected by sin.

If it were asked whether the historical school has not at least provided us with a clear criterion whereby we may distinguish between progressive and reactionary tendencies in the cultural process, the answer must be in the negative. The reason is that its conception of historical development clings exclusively to biotic analogies in the modal structure of the historical aspect. Since this aspect is definitely founded in that of organic life, these biotic analogies cannot fail to reveal themselves in the modal sense of the historical idea of development. Cultural movement and development are inherent in cultural life, and consequently von Savigny's distinction between living and dead elements in the historical tradition of a nation is well founded. The historical sense of this distinction is qualified by the nuclear moment of the historic-cultural mode of experience. Living elements are those which still have formative power in a human community, whereas dead elements are those which have definitely lost that power, and in the future only have a folkloristic or a merely theoretical historical importance.

But these biotic analogies are of a retrospective character. They refer backwards in order of time to an earlier aspect of our experiential horizon which lacks a normative character. Development in the modal sense of organic life, which is based upon physico-chemical processes, is not ruled by norms, but by biotic laws of nature. In the biotic aspect of time the development of a multicellular living organism displays only the natural phases of birth, growth, maturing, ageing, and decline. But in historical development a normative human vocation reveals itself, a cultural task entrusted to humankind at the creation. This task cannot be fulfilled except in the anticipatory direction of time, in which the historico-cultural aspect of the temporal deepens its modal meaning by unfolding its anticipatory moments in referring forwards to post-historical aspects.

Therefore the nuclear moment of the cultural mode of development, i.e., formative power, has itself a normative sense since it implies a normative cultural vocation, as is apparent from the divine cultural command to subdue the earth. Even the most terrible misuse of power in our sinful world cannot make power itself sinful, nor can it detract from the normative sense of a person's cultural vocation.

### The anticipatory meaning of the cultural-historical aspect

Until the cultural aspect of a human community discloses the anticipatory moments of its meaning, it shows itself to be in a rigid and primitive condition. The same holds good for those normative aspects which are

founded in the cultural, i.e., the linguistic aspect of symbolic signification, the aspect of social interaction, the economic, aesthetic, juridical,
and moral aspects, and the aspect of faith. Primitive cultures are confined
to small and undifferentiated communities which display a strong tendency towards isolation. As long as such primitive communities maintain their isolation in history there can be no question of cultural development in the sense in which it is taken in historiography proper.

They display a totalitarian aspect, since they involve themselves in all
spheres of their members' personal lives, while the temporal existence of
the individual is completely dependent on membership of the family or
sib respectively and of the tribal community. There is no room yet for a
differentiation of culture in the particular spheres of formative power,
i.e., those of science, the fine arts, commerce and industry, politics, religion, and so on. Since such undifferentiated communities fulfil all the
tasks for the purpose of which, on a higher level of civilization particular
organizations are formed, there is only one single undifferentiated cultural sphere. A rigid tradition, deified by a pagan belief, and anxiously
guarded by the leaders of the group, has the monopoly of formative
power. The process by which such cultures are developed shows, in fact,
only biotic analogies of the phases of birth, growth, maturing, ageing,
and decline. The duration of such culture's existence is dependent on that
of the small popular or tribal communities by which they are sustained.
They may vanish from the scene without leaving any trace in the history
of humankind.

The situation in the historical development of opened-up cultures is
quite different. From the ancient cultural centers of world history, such
as Babylon, Egypt, Palestine, Crete, Greece, Rome, Byzantium, essential
tendencies of development passed over into medieval and modern Western civilizations. They fertilized the Germanic and Arabian cultures and
this fertilization has given rise to new forms of civilization. This opened-
up cultural development has been freed from rigid dependence upon the
living conditions of small popular or tribal communities. It does not
move within the narrow bounds of a closed and undifferentiated cultural
community, but, like a life-giving stream, it always seeks new channels
along which to continue its course.

The process whereby a culture is opened up always occurs in a conflict
between the guardians of tradition and the propounders of new ideas.
The formative power of tradition is enormous, for in a concentrated form
it embodies cultural treasures amassed in the course of centuries. Every
generation is historically bound to former generations by its tradition.
We are all dominated by it to a much greater degree than we realize. In a
primitive closed culture its power is nearly absolute. In an opened-up

culture, tradition is no longer unassailable but it has the indispensable role of guarding that measure of continuity in the cultural development without which cultural life would be impossible.

In the struggle with the power of tradition the progressive ideas of so called moulders of history themselves have to be purged of their revolutionary subjectivity and adjusted to the modal norm of historical continuity. Even Jacob Burckhardt, who was strongly affected by historicistic relativism, held to this norm of continuity as a last guarantee against the decline of all civilization. It is, of course, nothing but an illusion to imagine that a cultural revolution can destroy all bonds with the past and begin with the revolutionary year one.

This opening-up process of culture is characterized by the destruction of the undifferentiated and exclusive power of primitive communities. It is a process of cultural differentiation which is balanced by an increasing cultural integration. It is effected by the bursting of the rigid walls of isolation which have enclosed the primitive culture and by submitting the latter to fruitful contact with civilizations which have already been opened up.

Since Herbert Spencer (societal) differentiation and integration has been accepted by many sociologists as a criterion for distinguishing between more highly developed and primitive societies. The process of differentiation was viewed as a consequence of division of labour, and an attempt was made to explain it in a natural scientific manner. But I do not understand the term "cultural differentiation" in this pseudo-natural scientific sense.

What I have in mind instead is a differentiation in the typical individuality-structures of social relationships. In the cultural-historical aspect of these relationships this process of differentiation finds expression in the rise of a rich diversity of typical cultural spheres, each of which is characterized by a leading function of a distinct normative modality belonging to a post-historical aspect of experience. Differentiated cultural spheres, such as those of science, the fine arts, commerce and industry, politics, religion, and so on, can be realized only on the basis of the opening-up process of history. But this does not mean that their typical individuality-structures are themselves of a variable historical character. Since these structures determine the inner nature of the differentiated relationships of society and their typical cultural spheres they must belong to the order of creation in its temporal diversity, which is also the order of our experiential horizon. It is only the social forms in which they are realized that vary in the process of historical development.

The irrationalistic trend in historicism started from the position of the absolute individuality of any socio-cultural community. But this trend overlooked the typical individuality-structures which determine the inner total nature of these communities and which, as such, cannot be of a variable historical character. Nevertheless, it is true that the process of increasing cultural differentiation and integration is at the same time a process of increasing individualization of human culture, in so far as it is only in a culture which has been opened up and differentiated that individuality assumes a really historical significance. It is true that in a primitive closed cultural sphere individuality is not lacking. But in consequence of the rigid dominance of tradition this individuality retains a certain traditional uniformity, so that from generation to generation such closed cultures in general display the same individual features. It is for this reason that historiography in its true sense takes no interest in these cultural individualities.

As soon, however, as the process of differentiation and integration commences, the historical task to bring individual cultural dispositions and talents to fruition becomes manifest. Every individual contribution to the opening up of the cultural aspect of human society is a contribution to the cultural development of humankind which has a world-encompassing perspective. Accordingly the individuality of cultural leaders and groups assumes a deepened historical sense.

It is the opening-up process of human culture also which alone can give rise to national individualities. A nation viewed as a socio-cultural unit should be sharply distinguished from the primitive ethnical unity which is called a popular or tribal community. A real national cultural whole is not a natural product of blood and soil, but the result of a process of differentiation and integration in the cultural formation of human society. In a national community all ethnical differences between the various groups of a population are integrated into a new individual whole which lacks the undifferentiated totalitarian traits of a closed and primitive unit of society.

It was, therefore, unmistakable proof of the reactionary character of the Nazi myth of blood and soil that it tried to undermine the national consciousness of the Germanic peoples by reviving the primitive ethnic idea of "folk" (*"Volkstum"*). Similarly, it is unmistakable proof of the retrograde tendency of all modern totalitarian political systems that they attempt to annihilate the process of cultural differentiation and individualization by a methodical mental equalizing (*"Gleichschaltung"*) of all cultural spheres, thereby implying a fundamental denial of the value of the individual personality in the opening-up process of history.

The counter-revolutionary political movement in the first half of the nineteenth century which strove for a restoration of the feudal regime in its broader sense, with its undifferentiated patrimonial conception of political authority was doubtless also of a reactionary character. It wished to restore a political system which was incompatible with the idea of the state and the implied integration of a nation. For this reason it was doomed to disappear as soon as the state was realized in the progressive line of politico-historical development. In the opening-up process of history upholding any undifferentiated remnants of political power-formation should be overcome since it contradicts the norm of politico-historical differentiation and integration. This norm, however, is not of a merely *modal* historical character since it is oriented to the typical structural principle of the state as a *res publica* which in its historical aspect implies a monopolistic organization of the power of the sword, serviceable in the public interest of the body politic.

Because the opening-up process of the cultural-historical aspect occurs in the anticipatory or progressive direction of the temporal order, it must be possible to indicate the anticipatory moments in which the dynamic coherence of meaning between this aspect and the subsequently arranged normative modes reveals itself. To begin with, the progressive opening-up process of history is characterized by the manifestation of a linguistic anticipation. The *linguistic* aspect of our experiential horizon is that of communication by the medium of signs which have a symbolic meaning. In the opening-up process of historical development, facts assume a historical significance which give rise to a symbolical signification of their historical meaning.

Hegel and von Ranke held that history in its true sense did not start before the need arose to preserve the memory of historical events by means of chronicles, records and other materials. The so called *Kulturkreislehre* in ethnology, which seeks to trace genetic continuity in the cultural life of humankind from the so called primeval cultures of pre-history on to civilizations at the highest level of development, has denied that the presence of memorials can be of any essential importance for the delimitation of the historical field of research. As Frobenius has said, history is action, and in comparison with that reality how inessential is its symbolical recording!

The truth is, however, that such a depreciation of the rise of historical memorials as regards their significance for the historical development of humankind testifies to a lack of insight into the modal structure of the opening-up process of culture. For the rise of such memorials is an unquestionable criterion of the historical opening up of a civilization. It cannot be inessential that in primitive societies historical memorials, or at least reliable oral forms of historical information, are lacking and that only mythological representations of the genesis and development of their culture are found. The relatively uniform course of their process of development has not yet provided *Mnemosyne*[1] i.e., any memorable, historically significant material worth recording. An as yet closed historical consciousness clings to the biotic analogies in cultural development and inclines to a mythological interpretation of its course under the influence of a primitive religion of nature.

The manifestation of symbolical or linguistic anticipation in the opening-up process of the historical aspect of experience is indissolubly linked to a manifestation of cultural intercourse between different nations which are caught up in the stream of world history. Cultural intercourse in this international sense is an anticipatory moment in history referring forwards to the opening up of the modal aspect of social interaction with its specific norms of good manners, courtesy, and so on. A manifestation of such cultural intercourse means that a national culture is opened up to the formative power of foreign cultural activity, so that there is a continuous mutual exchange of cultural life between the nations. Since without such a free cultural intercourse the historical opening-up process cannot make headway, any attempt by a totalitarian regime to impede or exclude this free cultural contact must be considered reactionary. The normative criterion lying at the foundation of this judgment is not of a merely subjective character since it proves to be rooted in the modal structure of the historical opening-up process. This may be verified by observing the consequences of cultural isolation for a highly developed nation. It is for this reason that such reactionary measures of a totalitarian regime cannot be sustained in the long run.

Since the process of cultural differentiation leads to an increasingly typical diversity of cultural spheres, there is a constant danger that one of these spheres may try to expand its formative power in an excessive manner at the expense of the others. Indeed, since the dissolution of the ecclesiastically unified culture which prevailed in medieval Western civilization there has been a running battle between the emancipated cultural spheres to acquire supremacy over each other.

In the opening-up process of history, therefore, the preservation of a harmonious relationship between the differentiated spheres of culture becomes a vital interest of the entire human society. But this cultural harmony can be guaranteed only if the process of historical development complies with the normative principle of cultural economy which forbids any excessive expansion of the formative power of a particular sphere at the expense of the others. Here the aesthetic and economic anticipations in the historical aspect reveal themselves in their unbreakable inner coherence. Both principles, that of cultural economy and that of cultural harmony, appeal to the inner nature of the differentiated cultural spheres

---

1   *Memory* – Translator.

as determined by the typical individuality-structures of the circles of society to which they belong. It is my conviction that these individuality-structures are based upon the order of creation, whereby due bounds are assigned to every temporal entity in accordance with its nature.

As soon as these bounds are ignored in the opening-up process of human culture through an excessive expansion of the formative power of a particular cultural sphere, disastrous tensions and conflicts arise in human society. This may evoke convulsive reactions on the part of those cultural spheres which are threatened, or it may even lead to the complete ruin of a civilization, unless counter-tendencies in the process of development manifest themselves before it is too late and acquire sufficient cultural power to check the excessive expansion of power of a particular cultural factor.

It is in such consequences of the violation of the principles of cultural economy and harmony in the historical opening-up process that a juridical anticipation in history comes to light. At this point we find ourselves confronted with the Hegelian utterance: *"die Weltgeschichte ist das Weltgericht" (world history is world judgment)*. I do not accept this dictum in the sense in which Hegel meant it; but that the violation of the normative principles to which the opening-up process of the cultural aspect of history is subject is avenged in the course of world history may be verified by observing the consequences of such violation.

When finally the question is asked: "what is the deepest cause of disharmony in the opening-up process of history?" we come face to face with the problem concerning the relationship between faith and culture and with the religious basic motives which operate in the central sphere of human life. The disharmony in question belongs, alas, to the progressive line of cultural development, since it can only reveal itself in the historical opening-up process of cultural differentiation. In a primitive closed culture the conflicts and tensions, which in particular are to be observed in modern Western civilization, cannot occur. As a consequence of the fact that any expansion of the formative power of humankind gives rise to an increasing manifestation of human sin, the historical opening-up process is marked by blood and tears, and does not lead to an earthly paradise.

What, then, is the sense in all this extreme endeavor, conflict, and misery to which people submit themselves in order to fulfil their cultural task in the world? Radical historicism, as it manifested itself in all its consequences in Spengler's *Decline of the West*, deprived the history of humankind of any hope for the future and made it meaningless. This is the result of the absolutization of the historical aspect of experience. For we have seen that the latter can only reveal its significance in an unbreakable coherence with all the other aspects of our temporal horizon of experience. And this horizon itself points at the human ego as its central locus of reference, both in its spiritual communion with all other human egos and in its central relationship to the Divine Author of all that has been created.

In the final analysis the problem of the meaning of history revolves around the central question of who are human beings themselves and what is their origin and their final destination? Outside of the biblical basic motive of creation, fall, and redemption through Jesus Christ, no real answer is, in my opinion, to be found to this question. The conflicts and dialectical tensions which occur in the process of the opening-up of human culture result from the absolutization of what is relative. And every absolutization takes its origin from the spirit of apostasy, from the spirit of the *civitas terrena*, as Augustine called it.

There would be no future hope for humankind and for the whole process of human cultural development, if Jesus Christ had not become the center of world history. This center is bound neither to the Western nor to any other civilization, but it will lead the new humankind as a whole to its true destination, since it has conquered the world by the love revealed in its self-sacrifice.

# The dangers of the intellectual disarmament of Christianity in Science[1]

## "Objective Science" and "Subjective Faith"

SCIENCE[2] IS A FIELD for which, at first glance, the Christian faith appears to have less relevance than for any other field. This is true if one restricts the concept of science to the systematic and methodical investigation of what is given objectively within the bounds of universally valid human experience. People will try to enhance the status of many activities by claiming for them the designation of "science" when in fact they are not entitled to do so if measured by the aforementioned criterion. Examples are Metaphysics, which focuses on the hidden foundation of the world of experience, and Dogmatic Theology. But for these activities the false label of "science" cannot change the nature of the goods offered. To be sure, Metaphysics and Dogmatic Theology engage in theoretical and scientific forms of thought. But in this context these thought forms lack scientific content because they are used in separation from the objective coherence of experience. Hence, they become lost in the vacant, empty spaces of speculation.

This does not mean that science is unable to satisfy the deepest needs of the human heart. On the contrary! Those who so jealously try to delimit the boundaries of science from faith and who reject any intrusion by faith into "autonomous" scientific research are usually the last to deny the innate value of faith. But, they claim, faith is not focused on the

---

1 This essay constitutes chapter IV, *De gevaren van de geestelijke ontwapening der Christenheid op het gebied van de Wetenschap* in the volume entitled *Geestelijk Weerloos of Weerbaar?* (Intellectually Defenceless or Armored?), introduced by J.H. DeGoede Jr., Ed. (Publisher not identified, Amsterdam, 1937, pp. 153-212). Translator: *John Vriend*; Editors: *T. Grady Spires, Natexa Verbrugge, Magnus Verbrugge*.

2 *Editorial note* (DFMS): The Dutch term "wetenschap" has a broader scope than what the word "science" if often associated with in English. "Wetenschap" refers to all the academic disciplines, not merely to the natural sciences such as mathematics and physics.

general reality of experience. Thus the contents of faith cannot be verified by universally valid scientific criteria. They must remain a matter of personal conviction, which admittedly is worthy of respect, but nonetheless completely subjective.

According to this view, there could be no worse compromise of the Christian faith than to make it the judge over science, or somehow make it the foundation of scientific inquiry in the claim for a Christian science. As soon as the boundaries between them are erased, faith and science must turn into irreconcilable adversaries. Only complete separation will allow them to co-exist in peace and even in harmony.

After Immanuel Kant developed the principles of his "critical" philosophy, this line of thought became so dominant in science that it seemed utterly futile to tamper with it. Also in protestant Christian circles resistance to this so-called critical view of science weakened visibly. Here only dogmatic theology remained a problem, because it in no way allowed itself to be forced into the framework of the dominant concept of science. After all, by means of his critical method of thought, Kant had apparently dismantled it completely and denied it any right to exist as science.

Humanists still tried to save the scientific character of theology by construing "religious experience" as a unique area within the contents of consciousness. But in the bounds of the ruling view of science, this was only possible by ascribing a purely psychological character to this "religious experience." In other words, faith had to be dethroned and reduced to a verifiable psychic complex of feelings accessible for exact scientific description. However, this meant that faith had to be completely detached from its orientation to a supra-temporal divine Truth. Such an "empirical" analysis of the life of faith thus had to buy its scientific credentials at the price of every link with Christian dogma. It thus had to consent to being reduced to a "psychology of religion." As such it could rank alongside an ethnology of the religious notions of primitive peoples and a critical historical inquiry into the religious ideas of the "cultured" nations – Christian nations in particular.

Along neo-Kantian lines, one could also develop a "critical" theology, which could investigate the "universally valid forms" of religious experience. Alternatively, theology could be diluted into a critical moral philosophy.

It goes without saying that such a conception of theological science could never be accepted by true confessing Christians. Those that were influenced by the dominant view of the separation of faith and science continued to maintain a special position for theology that was hard to defend. The inevitable result was a relentless conflict between the so-called secular sciences and sacred theology (sancta theologia). In the end, this conflict could only lead to internal estrangement between Christian special scientists and Christian dogmatic theologians.

## The separation between the special sciences and philosophy

In Christian circles, a second factor emerged which strongly reinforced the overpowering influence of the prevailing view of science, namely, the generally uncritical acceptance of the separation between the special sciences and philosophy that had developed in humanistic thought.

Essentially, philosophy is theoretical reflection on the origin, the central unity, and the mutual relationship and coherence of all those aspects of temporal reality that are selected by the special sciences as separate fields of study. It also includes the theoretical examination of the diverse individuality-structures within which temporal reality offers itself to human experience.[1]

## A blind faith in the sovereignty of human reason

In its scientific attitude toward reality, philosophy may never be confused with a person's *pre*scientific world view. Nevertheless, understood in the above sense, philosophy is inseparably bound up with the latter, both in its starting point and in its orientation. Its focus on the Origin and the deeper central unity of created reality must lead to theoretical reflection on the principles and presuppositions of scientific activity itself. In this process, philosophy must deal with the question of whether science as such is intrinsically self-sufficient, or whether its essential presuppositions are supra-theoretical in nature.

It is not hard to see that philosophy, by dogmatically maintaining that theoretical thought is absolutely self-sufficient vis-a-vis faith, imprisons itself in a blind faith in the sovereignty of human reason. In other words, in this case it uncritically and unscientifically refuses to give a theoretical account of its own most basic presuppositions.

Now, this truly uncritical and dogmatic attitude of thought did try to look critical by attempting to show that every attack on the postulate of the intrinsic self-sufficiency of theoretical thought undermines the foundations of science. It was argued that philosophy, if in fact it is to remain truly scientific, has to restrict itself to critical examination of the universally valid conditions of human knowledge. As a science, it should only search for theoretical truth; it must bring to light the absoluteness and

---

1  Regarding what follows see my: *"De Wijsbegeerte der Wetsidee,"* Book I (Paris, Amsterdam 1935), Prolegomena; and the first volume of my *A New Critique of Theoretical Thought* (Collected Works, A-Series, Mellen Press, Volumes, 1-4).

self-sufficiency of this theoretical truth by showing that every attempt to relativize the latter, by positing its dependence on some extra-scientific matter of faith, necessarily leads to a skeptical relativism that internally refutes itself.

Theoretical truth, it was argued, possesses its own inner warrant for its self-sufficiency, its independence from other values in life. This is not a question of faith (e.g. according to the neo-Kantian philosopher Heinrich Rickert), but rather something that can be demonstrated in a rigorous logical manner.

As soon as someone expresses the judgement that "theoretical truth is not universally valid," that person claims universal validity, i.e. theoretical truth, for the judgement itself. In other words, he or she immediately contradicts the meaning of his or her own opinion and implicitly acknowledges the universal validity of truth.

This viewpoint did not see that this whole line of reasoning completely misses the mark. Rather it leads to making truth relative to imagined purely scientific thinking. Indeed, in the name of absolute Truth, the claim was made for an intrinsically impossible self-sufficiency of theoretical thought. Nonetheless, this claim also impressed Christian philosophers.

Thus as soon as philosophic thought was declared self-sufficient within its own domain, the fundamental line of demarcation between philosophy and the special sciences no longer seemed to present any difficulties.

Philosophy was not to interfere with the activity of the special sciences in the investigation of empirical reality. Instead, insofar as it is a theory of science, it must restrict itself to an inquiry into the immanent presuppositions of scientific activity as such, i.e., into the universally valid forms of knowledge which first make science possible. In other words, it must restrict itself to *epistemology.*

This whole train of thought was again dogmatically based on the self-sufficiency of the special sciences, each within its own field, just as they in fact had developed under the influence of Humanism. People spoke of the factual reality of science ("Faktum der Wissenschaft"), which philosophy would simply have to accept as such, since philosophy had no right whatsoever to a voice in the internal process of scientific research.

In the special sciences themselves, a strong positivistic trend gained the upper hand. As a reaction against speculative philosophy, which sought to impose its aprioristic deductions on reality, scientists believed they could completely emancipate themselves from philosophy and restrict themselves to an unbiased examination of factual phenomena without accounting for their meaning.

Based on this view of philosophy and science, it is indeed impossible to speak meaningfully about Christian science in any way. For the special sciences only have to stick to the "objective facts," which should be examined according to universally valid, completely objective scientific methods. On that basis philosophy is nothing other than scientific thought's critical, theoretical self-reflection on its own purely theoretical activity. Even when people once again understood the task of philosophy to be universal and wanted to expand it into a world view, they maintained the purely theoretical attitude that excluded all standards of faith as the *conditio sine qua non* for its scientific character. What else then could the Christian faith really have to do with science?

## Kuyper and the idea of a twofold Science

Given the supremacy of this concept of science, it is understandable that only a few people, even in Christian circles, took seriously the antithesis posited by Dr. Abraham Kuyper between a science that arises from the rebirth [in Christ] and one that is the fruit of the apostate root of creation.

The founding of the Free University of Amsterdam, as an outgrowth of this idea of the antithesis, was greeted with thinly veiled derision. At best, this was seen as a superficial linking of scientific research to dogmatic theology, which itself has nothing to do with real science. In later years, even some like-minded academics who were close to Kuyper began to doubt the possibility of a genuinely Christian science. For many of them, the arguments for the necessity of a strictly factual science, ostensibly not bound by any dogmatic presuppositions of faith, proved too strong. Since they imagined that the case for a genuinely Christian science was already lost, they demanded a new awareness of the relationship between the kingdom of Christ and secular culture, particularly the relationship between Christian faith and science. They looked for a theological basis for a dualistic standpoint which could ultimately justify, even to the Christian conscience, the factual neutrality of science vis-a-vis the Christian faith.

In this spirit, an appeal was made to the doctrine of common grace. This doctrine was now being interpreted in such a way that a natural dividing line between faith and unbelief in the "domain of common grace" cannot exist. Rather, such a line is given only in the "domain of special grace." After all, so they reasoned, Christ's kingdom is not of this world, but natural knowledge is the common property of believers and unbelievers. Even the Christian can serve God in this area without surrendering to the impossible ideal of a Christian science.

The divine Word revelation, they argued, is directed not at scientific thought but at faith. It can never embrace anything that human reason must track down by way of strict scientific research. Science, belonging as it does to the domain of common grace, is *factually* independent of Christ's kingdom. Within its own sphere, it contributes to the glory of God, Who after all has bestowed science to humankind as a gift of common grace. The Christian faith only affects Christian scientists to the extent that they accept their factually neutral scientific activity as a task for the glory of God.

I think that this line of thought had already thoroughly affected many Christian scientists before dialectical theology, under the leadership of Karl Barth and Emil Brunner, launched its fierce systematic attack on the idea of a Christian science. This attack was all the more serious because this time it came not from the humanistic camp, but rather from a quarter which at the same time wanted to call theology back to the Word of God with prophetic fervor.

Since I have just spoken of a systematic attack on the idea of Christian scholarship, I now intend to define the meaning of these words.

**The approach of Emil Brunner**

Apparently Emil Brunner, whose standpoint I especially wish to discuss here, does not teach a division in any sense between science and Christian faith. In the face of the prevailing humanistic view, he defends the scientific character of Christian theology and ethics, which are subjected to the Word of God. He emphatically opposes the humanistic notion of a self-contained and absolutely self-sufficient reason. On the contrary, he maintains, reason must be imbued with faith. In this way the Christian will see the world of reason (*Vernunftwelt*) in a new light through the Word of God.[1]

Nevertheless, Brunner does consciously say that "a scientist should not conduct his research as a Christian but as a scientist ... – ..."[2] With this he means to emphasize that the Christian faith can have no constitutive, materially constructive significance for scientific research, inasmuch as science focuses on temporal reality governed by its own laws. So in the immanent course of this research, Christian science is irrelevant.

In this line of thought there is no place either for a Christian philosophy as I described earlier. In philosophy, too, the faith of the Christian thinker remains merely a regulative and critical principle, meant to protect him from "rationalistic digressions and speculative overstepping of boundaries."[3] However, in its internal operations, philosophic thought remains unaffected by this principle. The notion that philosophy from a

---

1  Cf. *Das Gebot und die Ordnungen* (1932), p.76.

2  *Op.cit.*, p.246.

3  *Op.cit.*, p.664, note 470.

Christian standpoint should develop its own insight into the structure of reality, the structure of human knowledge, the formation of concepts, etc., is excluded in principle by Brunner's entire view of the relationship between Christian faith and temporal existence. Only where the real root, the real center of human existence, of the human personality, is at stake does the Christian faith have a positive contribution to make to science. For this center exists only in a direct personal relationship to God, as it has been essentially tainted by the fall into sin, just as it has been redirected to God through Christ. Science cannot lead to genuine self-knowledge. Indeed, insofar as natural thought tries to reach this knowledge on its own, it lapses into false speculations that are unmasked and unraveled by the Word of God as learned through faith.

It is not hard to see that, for the Christian, an inner reconciliation between faith and science from this standpoint is out of the question. To be sure, the humanistic separation is rejected, and the humanistic concept of science is penetrated to the extent that room is made for Christian theology and ethics. However, the objective arbitrariness of science, oriented to temporal reality, is given an emphatically greater validity than the Christian faith. And it is represented in such a way that any other conception means essentially an attack on the spirit of the Reformation, indeed, an assault on the Christian faith itself.

In earlier discussions I have already shown that underlying this dualistic standpoint there is an essentially un-Christian scheme of thought. Already early on, Christian thought was penetrated by a contrast between nature and grace, overshadowing the scriptural antithesis between the fall and redemption, the kingdom of darkness and the kingdom of Christ. Originally, the nature-grace scheme served to effect a synthesis, a compromise, between the Christian doctrine of faith and pagan thought.

Nature came to be identified with the temporal structure of God's creation as it was conceived in the light of Greek philosophy, and an attempt was made to adapt this concept to the divine Word-revelation. Initially, under the influence of Augustine, natural reason was regarded as incapable of arriving at true knowledge of the cosmos without the light of the divine Word-revelation.

### Aristotle and Thomas Aquinas: Nature and Grace

Much later, Thomas Aquinas (1225-1274), the grand-duke of medieval scholasticism, boldly dared to declare human reason autonomous and self-sufficient in its own domain, i.e. that of "natural" knowledge. In other words, he emancipated human reason from the divine Word-revelation in Christ Jesus.

Still, Thomas did not teach the absolute self-sufficiency of natural reason either. Rather, he took the typically Roman Catholic position that nature is a lower stage preceding grace, in the sense that it has to be brought by grace to a subsequent higher, and this time indeed Christian, level of perfection. This position implied the equally typical Roman Catholic idea that the fall has not radically corrupted nature. Sin merely caused it to lose the "supra-natural" gift of grace, which undoubtedly "wounded" the "nature" of creation. Since then Thomas' doctrine of the autonomy of natural reason within its own domain has never disappeared from Christian thought.

It soon became apparent, however, that the compromise found in the Thomistic system between the Christian doctrine of faith and pagan philosophy could not mean an inner reconciliation between the two. Instead, it introduced an extremely dangerous internal rupture into Christian thought.

The philosophic conception of nature, construed as a stepping stone for Christian grace as accepted by Thomas, was essentially that of the Greek philosopher Aristotle. Aristotle, it must be noted, started out with an absolutization, essentially a deification, of reason. According to Aristotle, the temporal cosmos is rational in origin. God himself is absolute, pure, self-contained Reason.

Aristotle's conception of human nature is also entirely in keeping with this idea of the Origin of the temporal cosmos. In his view human nature has its supra-temporal root and center in the rational part of the soul. The latter is thought of as immortal as such, as the substance or essential form of all human existence. Its connection to the sensory and bodily functions is not essential to its structure. This view lifted the rational functions of being human out of their cosmic coherence with all other functions of its temporal existence. In a fundamentally false way, they were proclaimed to be the real supra-temporal center of human existence.

Now, this view was in irreconcilable conflict with the divine Word-revelation in Holy Scripture. For Scripture teaches us that, underlying all temporal functions of human existence, including rational functions, lies the heart, i.e., the real *selfhood*, the *religious root* from which all temporal functions spring: "out of the heart [not reason] are the issues of life!" How then could this Aristotelian conception be accepted as a natural pedestal for the higher revelation of God's Word concerning the religious meaning of human existence?

**The attempted synthesis between Greek paganism
and Biblical Christianity**

Indeed, the Thomistic synthesis was bought at the cost of an intrinsic denaturation of the scriptural idea, which was no longer understood. The "heart," the religious center of human existence, was now either being construed in the sense of the temporal function of feeling, or else it was identified with the intellect, with reason.

Holy Scripture was then interpreted accordingly! In Paul's pronouncements in Romans 2:14-15, the words "the work of the law written in their hearts" were read as if there stood: "written in their natural reason."[1] In this way, some church fathers already preferred to justify a synthesis between Christian doctrine and pagan moral philosophy. The human "soul" was essentially conceived in Aristotelian fashion as an "immortal substance," although – unlike Aristotle – the sensory function was also relegated to the immortal part of a person. Some spoke of the "primacy of the intellect," to which a voluntaristic movement in scholasticism juxtaposed "the primacy of the will."

Along with Aristotle's view of the origin and central unity of human nature, they also accepted his entire pagan view of the structure of temporal reality, namely a hierarchy of lower and higher forms of being. In this hierarchy, each lower form served as a means, as material, for a higher form of being, and each thing contained its own developmental law within its own essential form.

The Aristotelian conception of natural moral law was accepted too. According to this view, the good is not good because God commands it; on the contrary, God *has to* command the good because it is based on reason. Thus the Scriptural idea of God's sovereignty as Creator was totally emasculated, because in the final analysis God was bound to creaturely standards of reason. This conception was called *realistic* because, along the lines of the speculative idealism of Greek philosophy, the "good" was taken to be a *rational* idea and was credited with objective reality.

So, along with Aristotle's Metaphysics, his physics, psychology, logic, ethics, and his political theory were accepted as well.

Also adopted from Greek philosophy was the thesis that the state is the complete natural community, of which all other natural social relationships can only be dependent parts. In other words, by following Aristotle's view of the temporal world-order, according to which all things

---

1 Cf. even Calvin's *Opera* 49, 38: "nec vero cordis nomen pro sede affectuum, sed tantum pro intellectu capitur," where he follows the conception that became generally accepted since Augustine. The fact that Calvin nonetheless did not in any way find the "essence" of being human in "reason" is demonstrated by Bohatec in his work: *Calvin und das Recht* (1934, p.6). Furthermore, in his *Institutio* (III, 2, 33) Calvin accuses the scholastics of having strayed from the biblical perspective in their view that faith is merely intellectual knowledge, for by doing so they did not realize that faith must be alive in one's heart.

are combined into an order of matter and form, means and ends, lower and higher, human society is viewed as the ultimate bond in which family, clan, village community, business organization, etc., are all merely equal but lower, subservient components.

This notion of the state as the overall bond of natural society was rooted in the pagan starting point as well. People did not see that all temporal forms of society, according to Holy Scripture, are *rooted in the* supra-temporal, religious *community* of the human race. Instead, in apostate fashion, they looked within temporal society itself for an overall bond and proclaimed the state to be it.

Just as people accepted Aristotle's view of the realm of nature, they also looked within the supra-natural realm of grace for a supreme *temporal* bond that would have to embrace the whole of Christian society in all its forms. They found this in the temporal institution of the church. Thus the latter was accorded a place above the state. In essence, it was identified with the genuinely supra-temporal body of Christ, the "invisible church," as the religious central community of humanity reborn in Jesus Christ. Thus, the Scriptural notion of the supra-temporal, totalitarian kingdom of God, the *Civitas Dei*, was replaced by the unscriptural doctrine that the temporal institution of the church is the overall bond of all that is Christian. And so the church was also entirely understood by way of analogy to the state.

All this was the result of the radical misconception that the Christian religion could ally itself with apostate philosophy. According to Thomas Aquinas, the natural light of reason could not come into conflict with the supra-natural light of divine Revelation. After all, nature was supposedly the foundation, the pedestal for grace. Thomas only overlooked that, according to Scripture, natural reason proceeds from the *heart*, the religious root of a person's existence, and that therefore the radical fall into sin, the apostasy of the heart, has also darkened reason and turned it away from Truth.

The Thomistic proclamation of the self-sufficiency of natural reason within its own domain meant a major, although certainly unintentional, step toward the intellectual disarmament of Christianity in the realm of science. "Nature" opened the floodgates for pagan concepts to invade Christian thought and caused an inner process of decay. This process was tempered only by the repudiation of the most patently anti-Scriptural concepts of Greek philosophy (e.g., the theory of the eternity of matter) and by subordinating natural knowledge to the knowledge of Revelation. Such a process of decay could not be stopped as long as there was no radical break with the efforts to synthesize Christian faith and apostate philosophy.

**The late medieval reaction of William of Occam**

In the late Middle Ages a strong reaction against the Thomistic synthesis asserted itself. Instead of a supposedly harmonious accommodation of pagan philosophy to divine Revelation, a radical dualism between the two was taught. This, however, by no means meant a break with the pagan view of the nature of creation. On the contrary, the nominalistic movement of late scholasticism, which turned against the Thomistic view under the leadership of the English Franciscan William of Occam (14th Century), made the unscriptural character of its view of science even more pronounced. This was done by denying any connection between natural reason and the light of divine Revelation.

The nominalists did realize that the Aristotelian-Thomistic doctrine of the rational origin of the temporal world-order was in radical conflict with the Scriptural teaching concerning God's absolute sovereignty as Creator. But they were guilty of denaturing this doctrine even further, by conceiving of God's sovereignty as Creator as an unfettered, despotic arbitrariness. In this way, the theory of the primacy of the will, which had already been defended by Thomas' contemporary [John] Duns Scotus, took an utterly nominalistic and positivistic turn.

Acceptance of this view required the divine world-order to be seen as a pure product of caprice. According to Occam, the moral law in particular was so little grounded in an immutable divine "reason" that God's will might just as well have sanctioned a moral law of egoism. This view obviously dispensed with the Aristotelian-Thomistic conception that every existing being is created with a supra-arbitrary, universal essential form or nature which is objectively grounded in a rational world-order and extends this being into immanent law.

In Thomas' view, these forms of being were "immanent ideas" that had a real existence, both in individual things and in divine reason. Late scholastic nominalism taught, however, that ideas or universal concepts (*universalia*) have no real existence whatsoever, either in the divine mind or in temporal things. On the contrary, they are mere subjective products of human consciousness, serving as shorthand for a multiplicity of individual things which they represent as "natural signs." Reality was viewed as totally individualistic. What late medieval nominalism was doing was merely to follow another line of thought in Greek philosophy in contrast to the traditional Platonic-Aristotelian one, i.e., the subjectivistic, individualistic line.

The nominalistic view of science at first gave rise to a strongly positivistic and anti-metaphysical tendency. The exploration of hidden ground, the origin and substance of things, was regarded as beyond the reach of science. Science was limited to logic, mathematics and the "experimental" sciences. In this way, Occam had already banished theology from the realm of science. For him, faith and science were mutually exclusive. They did not clash with each other for the simple reason that nowhere did they even come into contact with each other. Occam did not teach, as Thomas did, the supra-natural perfection of natural reason by faith. Rather, the realms of nature and grace were now separated by an abysmal chasm, and science therefore was totally withdrawn from Christ's kingdom.

This nominalistic separation of nature and grace paved the way for the modern humanistic conception of the absolute self-sufficiency of science in its own domain. Through its positivistic bias, nominalism became the forerunner of the modern positivistic attitude in the special sciences. It cleared the way for the notion that scientific research is essentially independent of every philosophic conception of the meaning of reality, of its underlying root and Origin, and that theoretical truth contains its own validity.

The absolute separation between natural reason and Christian faith led gradually to a secularization that extended even to the truths of the Christian faith. This secularization would later be consummated by Humanism.

Nominalism's erroneous individualistic and subjectivistic view of temporal reality spread to its theory of human society. Since it had decisively rejected the Thomistic construct of nature as the pedestal of grace, it naturally could no longer place the temporal institution of the church above natural society.

That is why nominalism took up battle on every front against the church's supremacy over the state, science, art, commerce, etc. By itself, this could have been welcomed as an acknowledgement of the intrinsic commonly shared independence of the relationships within society, were it not for the fact that nominalism viewed those relationships, emancipated from the church, as entirely independent from the kingdom of God in Christ Jesus as well. Society was construed from the supposedly independent individual. The rich diversity of structures, embedded by God in the temporal forms of society, was fundamentally erased by the uniform construction of social relationships using the willing consent of individuals who were by nature equal.

This line of thought would later form the basis for the ideas of the French revolution. In keeping with the nominalistic notion that every manifestation of law and order ultimately is a product of subjective arbitrariness, the authority of government and the official authority of the church were also construed from the "general will" (*volonté générale*) of the individuals who joined together in the social relationship.

## The rise of the Humanistic Science Ideal

In the sixteenth and seventeenth century, the modern nominalistic school of thought, which arose from the spirit of the Renaissance, laid the foundations of mathematical natural science. Humanism then soon began to develop an ideal of science that contained a new program. The entire temporal cosmos was to be constructed theoretically from simple elements, following a uniform mathematical natural scientific method.

This new ideal of science, which constituted a radical break with the Aristotelian Metaphysics of the essential forms of things, was inspired by the budding world-view of Humanism. In its origin, therefore, it was in no way neutral or religiously unbiased. This humanistic world-view was a secularization of the Christian faith, both with regard to the sovereignty of God as Creator and with regard to Christian freedom. It broke radically with the Scriptural conception of the heart as the supra-temporal center or religious root of human existence. Moreover, it returned to the pagan notion that the human personality finds its center in reason.

Humanism broke equally, however, with the medieval Thomistic idea that this "reason" is an objective essential form that is created into human nature and ordered in a metaphysical, organic hierarchy of lower and higher essential forms. This view did not proceed from a given world of objective ideas, which confront human reason and which it can only reflect in its concepts. Rather, in subjectivistic and nominalistic fashion, it proclaimed the creative sovereignty of subjective thought.

The philosophy of Descartes, in which the humanistic faith in the sovereignty of reason found its first systematic expression, began with a universal methodical doubt of the entire reality given in naive experience. Only in the *cogito*, that is, in subjective (mathematical) thought, did Descartes' method finally come to rest.

The British philosopher Thomas Hobbes began his philosophic investigations entirely in the same spirit with the thought-experiment, i.e. he systematically broke down the whole given cosmos. Then, in a theoretical creative process using the simplest mathematical methods, he reconstructed it as a logical coherence of thought which no longer displays irrational flaws.

At work underlying this application of humanistic thought is the humanistic faith in the sovereignty of the human personality, which refuses to be bound by any law that it has not imposed upon itself in strict autonomy.

Indeed, this humanistic ideal of personality is also the hidden religious root of the modern humanistic ideal of science, an ideal that is focused on the mastery of all temporal reality with the help of modern natural scientific thought. Thus, the sovereign freedom of personality would have to reveal itself in science as complete master of the entire cosmos.

The Christian confession of God's sovereignty as Creator has disappeared here in the face of an arrogant faith in the creative power of mathematical thought. Similarly, the Christian idea of the believer's freedom in Christ Jesus has been totally denatured into the idea of the sovereign freedom and self-determination of the human personality.

The new humanistic ideal of science is utterly incompatible with the acceptance of a divine world-order to which scientific thought remains bound and in which each aspect, each facet of meaning of temporal reality, is guaranteed its own peculiar structure and meaning, its own sphere-sovereignty within its own circle of divine laws, i.e, within its own law-sphere.

The acceptance of such a world-order is, after all, incompatible with the humanistic faith in the theoretical creative power of mathematical thought, incompatible with faith in the sovereignty of human reason.

Serious implementation of this ideal of science requires that natural scientific thought acknowledges only those limits to its creative theoretical process that it has posited for itself. And if sovereign thought itself determines the boundaries of its own theoretical constructions, then it stands sovereign above these boundaries and can overstep them. To the extent, then, that thought is willing to make theoretical distinctions between the various aspects of reality (such as number, space, motion, organic life, feeling), it presumes nevertheless to be able to construct their mutual relations and coherence in a rigorous logical structure that does not impair the sovereignty of human thought.

**The inherent tension between the Humanistic Ideal**
**of Personality and the Ideal of Science**
In other words, creative mathematical thought usurps the role of cosmic lawgiver. It sets out to build the cosmic world-order itself, in sovereign freedom.

Inherent in the humanistic ideal of science, therefore, is a peculiar trend of continuity [*continuiteitstendenz*]. This ideal continually strives towards a theoretical leveling of the cosmic boundaries of meaning between the distinct law-spheres in which the divine world-order has enclosed the various aspects of temporal reality and which are held in a temporal coherence of meaning by this very world-order. However, the consistent application of this ideal of science must of necessity lead directly to a basic contradiction, a fundamental antimony, between itself and its deeper root, i.e., the humanistic ideal of personality from which it has sprouted.

After all, the humanistic ideal of science does not recognize any cosmic boundaries for the elaboration of the natural scientific method.

A consistent application of this method would ultimately have to treat even the free human personality itself as a natural scientific mechanism. As a result, faith in the absolute autonomy and sovereign freedom of the personality would need to be unmasked as a delusion. Thus the ideal of science logically ends up abolishing the ideal of personality from which it had arisen.

Here we have found the clue to the fundamental antimony between natural necessity and moral freedom. This antinomy plays a major role in modern science, in which it has crystallized into a sharp conflict between two types of law with which scientific thought operates, i.e., natural law and norm. I must dwell on this point a bit longer because it relates to the concept of law in modern science and to the whole humanistic view of the structure of reality. To that end, I will first of all try to shed more light on the modern view of science in its contrast with the medieval Aristotelian-Thomistic view.

**The Concept of Law**

The Aristotelian-Thomistic concept of law was oriented to the previously mentioned metaphysical doctrine of essential substantial forms. Aristotle had derived his notion of essential forms from observing living organisms. Plants and animals grow from seeds, which already contain their natural forms "in a nutshell."

Plato, Aristotle's teacher, had taught that the forms of temporal things are copies of supra-temporal ideas, which are contained within a *topos noetos*, an intelligible, unchangeable world. There they lead a self-sufficient existence, completely divorced from the temporal, changeable things that have been patterned on these ideas. However, this rigid separation between the world of ideas and the world of sensory phenomena could not account for the temporal development and change of things.

Aristotle broke with the Platonic dualism between a static world of ideas and a changing world of phenomena. He brought Plato's ideas down from their transcendent isolation and converted them into immanent essential forms of temporal things. These immanent essential forms then were supposed to be the immanent causes of the development and change of these things at the same time. Aristotle thus conceived them as the hidden seeds of things, in which the mature forms were already germinally present. As such, these substantial forms were called the entelechies of things to emphasize that each thing contains a purposive principle of development which it strives by nature to realize. Everything strives by nature toward its own perfection; that is, it develops in accordance with its innate entelechy toward the mature form that is already germinally present in it.

In other words, this concept of the essential substantial form is intended to explain the internal structure of individual things in the full concreteness of their existence. Scientific activity, in the Aristotelian view, involves abstracting these essential forms from the sensory perception of things and in classifying the formal concepts thus gained in a scientific system.

The concept of law contained in the Artistotelian view of science thus focuses on the internal individuality structures of things. It is not oriented to the abstract aspects of reality that are explored by the modern special sciences.

These aspects of reality – those of number, space, motion, organic life, feeling, logical analysis, historical development, language, social interaction, economy, beautiful harmony, justice, morality, and faith – are naturally at the same time aspects of things. A tree has a numerical side, a spatial side, a kinematic side, a biotic side, a sensorially perceptible side, a logical conceptual side, a lingual side, etc.

**The universal functional framework of entities**

But within each aspect of reality, i.e. within each law-sphere of the temporal world-order, a law-governed functional coherence exists, which, as such, is independent of the inner structure of the things that function within it. For example, in the kinematic aspect of reality functional laws govern the motion of a pencil that I drop in my study as well as the movements of the planets in the universe.

In other words, in each aspect all things, regardless of their internal structure, cohere by functional laws. This functional coherence cannot be captured scientifically by means of the Aristotelian notion of substantial form. It can only be grasped in an abstract concept of function, which we deliberately abstract from the internal structure of individual things.

Modern physics does not operate with concepts such as animals, plants and mountains, but with the functional concepts of mathematically approximated mass in motion and of energy. This functional concept of law was unknown to Aristotle and to the men of the Middle Ages in their scientific investigation of natural phenomena. For example, they attributed the cause of the motion of falling objects to the inner nature (essential form) of heavy bodies, and they were not aware of the laws of gravity, which are universally valid for the entire physical aspect of the cosmos.

It was modern, mathematical natural science, founded by Galileo, that introduced the functional concept of law into physics. In so doing it pointed the way to the methodical control of natural phenomena. To that end, mathematical natural science had to radically banish the Aristotelian Metaphysics of hidden essential forms from the realm of physics.

Its concept of causality was no longer the Aristotelian notion of the internal purposive or formal cause (entelechy). Instead, it was the mathematically determined function concept which gathers all natural phenomena, in respect of their kinematic aspect,[1] under the same physical common denominator.

The humanistic ideal of science now seized upon this modern function concept in order to purge the entire cosmos, in all its dimensions of meaning, from "hidden qualities," and to construct it as an uninterrupted, continuous coherence of thought out of the simplest mathematical elements.

A functionalistic mode of thought began to appear in all the sciences. Thus the thought began to take hold that all other aspects of reality are only more complex modes or phenomenal forms of the mathematical or even the physical aspect.

In the process, organic life, feeling, historical development, language, social interaction, economics, etc., were eliminated as irreducible aspects

---

1  *Editorial note* (DFMS): Initially Dooyeweerd distinguished fourteen aspects only. In his first designation of the physical modality he used the term "movement" (cf. *De Wijsbegeerte der Wetsidee*, Vol.II, p.71: "den wetskring der beweging"). Eventually, after 1950, he realized that the science of kinematics (phoronomy) can "define a uniform movement without any reference to a causing force" – an insight which inspired him to distinguish between the *kinematical* and the *physical* aspects (cf. *A New Critique of Theoretical Thought* [NC], Vol.II, p.99). A noteworthy historical point in this connection is the fact that the brother-in-law of Dooyeweerd, the late professor D.H.Th. Vollenhoven, indeed introduced *fifteen* modalities in the first edition of his *Isagogé Philosophiae* in 1930 – by distinguishing the *mechanical* from the *physical* aspect. However, in the editions of 1936 and later this distinction vanishes because Vollenhoven then only acknowledges the physical aspect (cf. K.A. Bril: *A Selected and Annotated Bibliography of D.H.Th Vollenhoven*, in: *Philosophia Reformata*, 1973, p.216). Dooyeweerd, on the other hand, rightly mentioned the law of inertia as formulated by Galileo in this respect (cf. NC-II, p.99). That this law was anticipated by thinkers from the fourteenth century was convincingly shown by A. Maier (*Die Vorläufer Galileis im 14. Jahrhundert*, Roma 1949, pp.132-215). In a different context also P. Janich emphasized a "strict distinction between phoronomic (subsequently called kinematic) and dynamic statements" (*Tragheitsgesetz und Inertialsystem*, in: Frege und die moderne Grundlagenforschung, ed. Chr. Thiel, Meisenheim am Glan, 1975, p.68).

of meaning and conceived as mere modes or manifestations of the mathematical physical function. The modern functional concept of causality should then serve to make it possible to construe all of cosmic reality as a logically transparent, completely controlled coherence of thought. Entirely in keeping with this line of thought was the notion that even human society, even history, language, justice, etc., are nothing more than extremely complex applications of the laws of nature.

To this day the sciences of economics and sociology have not been fully liberated from this mechanistic conceptual framework. This functionalistic mode of thinking led to the radical leveling of the distinct modal aspects of reality as they are enclosed within their unique law-sphere; it also led to a fundamental elimination of all the individuality structures of things and of social relationships. I have already referred to the individualistic and leveling construction of human society in terms of the uniform scheme of the social contract.

The humanistic science-ideal imposed a particular view of the structure of reality on science, and it called this view the true, scientific one. Every other view was rejected as "mystical" or "mythological." The humanistic ideal of science had de-deified and de-spiritualized the cosmos.

## The Development of the Basic Antinomy in Humanistic Thought

Meanwhile, within the humanistic view of the cosmos the previously mentioned fundamental antimony between the ideal of science and the ideal of personality emerged. To maintain the latter, one could not allow the former to have unlimited scope. For, as we have seen, the ideal of science left no room for human freedom.

Already early on we thus find attempts to reconcile these two basic factors of the humanistic world-view by establishing boundaries for each. Descartes' strict separation of soul and body can be regarded as the first of these attempts.

For Descartes, the "body" was the sum of the mathematical, physical and biotic aspects of reality, all of which he brought together under the functional common denominator of physical space (extension). The "soul" was the sum of all the functions of human consciousness, which in turn were also reduced to the common denominator of mathematical thought.

Descartes then separated soul and body from each other as two "substances," requiring that the body be treated scientifically as though there were no soul, and the soul as though there were no body.

It is evident that behind this entire dualism lay Descartes' concern to protect the essence of the human personality (which he sought, in rationalistic fashion, in "creative mathematical thought") from being absorbed by the naturalistic ideal of science. For the latter wanted to dissolve all of reality in mechanistic causal relationships. Thought itself, at least, as the true seat of human freedom, had to be preserved.

By contrast, Thomas Hobbes, for instance, did not acknowledge any limits for the ideal of science. Thus the first conflict in humanistic philosophy arose between naturalism, which consistently applied the ideal of science, and semi-idealism, which tried to mark off a realm of ideal freedom for the human personality over against the trend of continuity in natural scientific thought.

Protestant Christian thought, which formerly had reached a compromise with the Aristotelian view of science, now generally compromised with the modern humanistic view. Thus Cartesian idealism gained influence also in Protestant theology. So now the church was forced to deal with a fresh set of heresies, which had originated in humanistic philosophy!

Pascal, who took his bearings entirely from Cartesian thought, tried to safeguard the Christian religion as a "matter of the heart" against the claims of modern thought and to depreciate the latter.

After a transitional phase, in the critical-positivistic skepticism of the Scottish philosopher David Hume, efforts to reconcile the modern ideals of science and personality finally led to Kant's critical view of science in the latter part of the eighteenth century. At the beginning of this essay I already referred to this view.

Kant depreciated the humanistic idea of science by strictly limiting science to sensorially perceptible phenomena. He radically rejected the humanistic Metaphysics that had emerged since Descartes, which believed that with the aid of modern mathematical thought it could reveal the "substance," the "true being," the supra-temporal root of reality.

Science, argued Kant, can only make known to us the "sensory world of phenomena." Furthermore, according to him this empirical reality is in fact nothing other than a coherence conforming to natural law in which theoretical thought reigns supreme. The "given" material of sensory experience is apprehended by human consciousness in *a priori* forms, and scientific thought then organizes it into a rigorous law-conformative coherence. This thought, however, remains bound to sensory perception. It cannot penetrate beyond sensory phenomena and provide knowledge of the substance, the "thing in itself" (*Ding an sich*).

Kant taught that behind the sensory world of phenomena there lurks a supra-sensory realm of freedom, where the human personality knows itself as an end in itself (*Selbstzweck*), a completely autonomous being. What is valid for this supra-sensory realm is not natural law, but the moral norm, the rule for what ought to be, whose objective is the free, moral self-determination of a person in action. This realm of freedom, however, can no longer be an object of scientific proof, but only of rational faith. Kant did not hesitate to ascribe primacy over the ideal of science to the ideal of personality, comprised in this rational faith.

The medieval scheme of nature and grace still attempted to synthesize pagan philosophy and the Christian doctrine of faith. Now, in the footsteps of Leibniz, this scheme was definitively replaced by the scheme of nature and freedom, which was totally focused on the here and now (*Diesseits*), on worldly life.

Since the rise of the humanistic ideal of science, the concept of nature had undergone a radical transformation. Kant had limited it to sensory phenomena, which natural scientific thought fashions into a rigorous coherence of natural law.

This nature, emptied of God or gods, now was equated with experiential reality. Science was to restrict itself to this reality so that its domain would be strictly marked off from questions of faith. The kingdom of grace was finally entirely secularized and humanized into a realm of the supra-sensory freedom of the human personality, which supposedly is at war with the lower sensory nature.

This Kantian so-called critical view of science also acquired great influence in Christian thought. We have already seen how it was viewed as the actual solution to the old conflict between science and Christian faith. After all, science had now definitely lost all rights to a voice in matters of faith. The Christian faith thus seemed so securely safeguarded from the attacks of science, to which it had been so exposed in the time of the Enlightenment!

Generally people realized that Kant's autonomous morality was unacceptable to a Christian. At the same time they fervently embraced all the more his critical view of experience and of the limits of science. Yet they completely failed to see that Kant's view of science ultimately sprang from the same religious root as his doctrine of autonomous morality.

They failed to see that his theory of science implied a perspective on the structure of reality in which the divine world-order had been banished as mythology. Nor did they see that this theory was dominated by a functionalistic, naturalistic way of thinking, based on the humanistic ideal of science.

In the meantime, humanistic philosophy did not stop with Kantian dualism. At first, the humanistic ideal of science had forced the ideal of personality to go on the defensive. Once Kant had assigned it priority in the humanistic world-view, however, it began to claim a monopoly in the theory of reality. For if, as we have seen, the typical continuity trend is peculiar to the ideal of science, the ideal of personality by virtue of its entire orientation cannot acknowledge any basic limits to its claims either.

People want to understand nature itself in the modern sense, as the domain of the humanistic ideal of science, as a product of the free personality, which Kant had conceived as a supra-sensory idea in a subjectivistic sense. Simultaneously, the earlier rationalistic, individualistic view of reality, still held by Kant, made way for an irrationalistic, universalistic view.

The former view saw reality, both in its sensory empirical and in its supra-sensory noumenal realms, essentially as a universal system of law. Individual subjectivity was then conceived of merely as a particular example of the law.

The latter view, on the other hand, which was just as one-sided, saw the essence of reality in subjective individuality. So, law as universal rule was valid merely as a thought form of the abstract, natural scientific point of view, which emasculates living reality.

People thought that they could only understand individuality by dialectical thought, that is, by taking the individual as a point of transition for a transpersonal, but equally subjective, individual totality.

As a result, in opposition to the atomizing and reductionistic mathematical, natural scientific way of thinking, a new method of thought was proposed, i.e., that of the humanities, which was to be focused on grasping the individuality as a whole. This method of thought is no longer oriented to mathematics and natural science, but rather to history with its individual wholes such as nation, people, cultural community, etc. Already in the *Sturm und Drang* period this new, irrationalistic view of reality began to challenge the absolutistic claims of the natural scientific view of reality.

Romanticism soon crowned the new, irrationalistic view as the only valid one. The dialectic method of thought accepted the humanistic conception's basic antinomy between natural necessity and freedom as a contradiction that is resolved within reality itself into a higher synthesis and harmony.

This method also controlled the monistic idealism of Hegel, who worked it out into a complete system of logic. Hegel sought to understand nature as a self-externalization of the idea, as a transitional phase in the dialectical self-unfolding of the absolute spirit.

### A new Attempt at Synthesis

Protestant Christian thought attempted to find a synthesis with these trends too. Christian Romanticism and Christian Hegelianism make their debut. Friedrich Julius Stahl was a well-known anti-revolutionary Lutheran thinker and statesman in Germany who had such a great influence on Groen Van Prinsterer [The Netherlands] in his second period. In his view of history even Stahl was strongly oriented to the romantic philosophy of Schelling and the irrationalistic Historical School.

Hence his identification of God's guidance in history with God's secret counsel, which is still accepted as a secondary norm for human action. Hence his notion that in the formation of law, common law (which supposedly evolves unconsciously under God's guidance) is holier in nature than deliberately enacted statutory law!

People did not see how the entire irrationalistic, dialectical conception of reality had its origin in an irrationalistic metamorphosis of the humanistic ideal of personality. Instead, they allowed their Christian thinking to become trapped in the humanistic law-idea's dilemma of nature and freedom. And they believed they could reinterpret the humanistic secularization of the Christian ideas of personality and freedom in a Christian way.

**The Reaction of Positivism**

Romanticism and Hegelianism started to introduce their speculative constructions into the various branches of the sciences as well. In the second half of the nineteenth century, this provoked a powerful reaction from these sciences against the interference by any philosophy of whatever type with "factual research."

This modern "positivistic" trend was not satisfied, however, with separating philosophy from the special sciences. At first it opposed all philosophy and identified it with speculation. Its proponents demanded a purely empirical mode of thought in science, one that would stick to the "facts."

Actually, this positivism was no more than a modern reaction of the naturalistic *ideal of science* against the romantic and idealistic Metaphysics of the humanistic *ideal of personality*. This reaction was clearly evident in the rise of Darwinism at that time. Darwinism changed the romantic organological and idealistic notion of development (which was oriented to the theory of history) in a mechanistic and individualistic sense. It acquired enormous influence in all the special sciences and even in psychology, the science of history, ethnology, economics, the theory of law, moral theory, and theology.

In his famous rectorial address entitled "Evolution," Abraham Kuyper depicted the overwhelming influence of Darwinian theories in this splendid opening: "The nineteenth century is fading away under the hypnosis of the dogma of Evolution."

Soon, the humanistic ideal of science built a new naturalistic philosophy (Haeckel, Buechner, and Moleschot) on the supposedly purely factual theory of evolution. And once more, Christian thought was looking for a compromise with the new dogma, particularly in the natural sciences. Holy Scripture's story of creation was placed in all manner of ways on the Procrustean bed of accommodation. Even some Christian students of nature failed to immediately recognize that the idea of a person having evolved from the lowest organisms in an unbroken, mechanical process of development was a naturalistic, speculative product of the humanistic ideal of science.

In the meantime, at the beginning of the twentieth century the inevitable reaction against this evolutionistic naturalism emerged. Ongoing scientific research provided not a single fact that confirmed the basic hypothesis of the Darwinian theory, i.e. that the real species, as completely variable forms, evolve in a continuous process of mechanical "adaptation."

**The cultural-historical method of the Humanities**

For their part, the humanities entered a protest against this evolutionistic interpretation of the facts. They demanded a method of research altogether different from that of the natural sciences, i.e. a "culture-historical" method, which would not seek to establish universal systems of law, but rather to understand strictly individual relationships.

As we have seen, the philosophical foundations for this method had already been laid by German idealism after Kant. However, the demand was no longer for an idealistic or romantic philosophy, but for a recognition of the unique character of the special scientific method of thought in the cultural sciences.

This whole development set humanistic epistemology in action once more. With the slogan "Back to Kant," a neo-Kantian philosophy emerged which began to focus particularly on a study of the universally valid, *a priori* (transcendental) conditions of all scientific knowledge.

Meanwhile, the real ideology of the humanistic ideal of personality, which Kant elaborated into a Metaphysics of rational faith, and which centered in the idea of freedom, had lapsed into a state of total decline under the overwhelming pressure of the positivistic school of thought.

At first, the neo-Kantians did not take into account the deepest root of the Kantian theory of science, i.e. a faith in the sovereign value of a person, or else they exchanged this rational faith for a skeptical relativism.

They confined their philosophical thought to a criticistic logical formalism whose only aim was to distinguish sharply between the *a priori* forms and the *empirical content* of scientific knowledge. *Science* had to be based on universally valid, *a priori* forms of consciousness in order to ensure its absolute independence from faith. Empirical research was assigned to the special sciences as an autonomous domain whilst critical epistemological reflection on the *a priori* forms of knowledge, operating in this research, was assigned to philosophy. In this manner an attempt was made to mark off the epistemological foundations of the new cultural historical method of research from those of mathematical natural science.

Heinrich Rickert in particular tried in this way to give a critical epistemological demonstration of the independent rights of the cultural sciences vis-a-vis the generalizing natural sciences.

Of course, this standpoint had to come into flagrant conflict with the recently developed Christian conception that the limits of the special sciences are determined by the divine world-order that has enclosed the various aspects of temporal reality in law-spheres, each of which is sovereign in its own area.

Much rather, in following the nominalistic line of Humanism, an attempt was made to find within the "epistemological consciousness" itself the formal difference demarcating the natural scientific from the cultural scientific mode of apprehending "empirical reality."

The neo-Kantian perspective on reality thus remained primarily oriented to the humanistic ideal of science. We noted earlier how Christian thought also began to fraternize with this neo-Kantian epistemology. It was considered a great gain to be able to put up a fight against the absolutistic claims of natural scientific thought with this epistemology; for ultimately these claims, besides leaving no room for a person's moral freedom and responsibility, did not leave any room for the Christian faith either.

**Irrationalistic historicism and relativism**

This neo-Kantian philosophy, which was basically a positivistic formalism, could not hold its ground for long. Its most dangerous enemy, the modern, irrationalistic existential philosophy, had already announced its presence before the outbreak of World War I. It gained the upper hand in philosophic thought through its revaluation of all values (*Umwertung aller Werte*), which we can observe today.

The spiritual fathers of this modern existential philosophy were Friedrich Nietzsche and the Danish theologian-philosopher Søren Kierkegaard. From the very outset this new movement in philosophy made its appearance in a variety of nuances.

Among the representatives of this movement was Wilhelm Dilthey, one of its most influential later thinkers, who focused on *historicism*.

Henri Bergson, the famous French professor, advocated a pronounced metaphysical *biologism*. The American pragmatist William James took a more *psychologistic* direction, and Martin Heidegger represented an *ontological-phenomenological* current.

The character of this entire existential philosophy of life is irrationalistic. Still, it cannot be regarded as a revival of the earlier romantic idealistic philosophy of life. Its main-stream, which is dominant today, arose out of a crisis in the foundations of the humanistic world-view. It passed through the modern positivistic process of decay. Faith in the ideal human personality had been the tradition in the metaphysical world of ideas. But two world views had already undermined it: on the one hand, the historical materialism of Marx, which was rapidly conquering the world of labor; on the other hand, empiricistic and neo-Kantian positivism.

Modern humankind lost all footholds for its world-view. It became conscious of the religious uprooting of its existence. The relativistic-historicistic criticism of Western culture (Oswald Spengler) predicted the imminent "decline of the West." Positivistic historicism gained ground and left no room for faith in eternal ideas.

The humanistic ideal of science in its older, metaphysical forms had undermined the humanistic idea of personality and freedom, but modern historicism affected this idea much more radically. Even the most sacrosanct ideas of the humanistic view of life were now treated as purely historical products of the mind, subject to the law of "rise, shine, and perish" in the ever-flowing stream of historical development.

The ancient Heraclitean maxim, *"panta rhei kai ouden menei"* (all is in flux, nothing abides), emerges here in human consciousness as a frightening reality. Indeed, even the humanistic ideal of science itself saw its foundations overturned by this historicism. Its relativizing nature left none of the old bulwarks standing. All that positivistic neo-Kantianism had managed to salvage from this tidal wave was merely a world of empty logical forms from which all material value had disappeared.

Hans Kelsen, the noted neo-Kantian legal theorist, hollowed out the Kantian concept of norm, which left it open to any arbitrary logical thought-form. He recklessly abandoned the natural-law idea of justice to the tide of relativism. The traditional humanistic idea of the constitutional state lost all axiological content in his thought; for he formalistically identified state and law and emasculated the law into a system of logical judgments, in which logical form alone was constant and supra-arbitrary.

The phenomenological movement in philosophic thought was founded by the well-known Göttingen professor Edmund Husserl. It is very influential in modern times. In its first strongly logicistic manifestation, it was also infected with the positivistic spirit. It subjected all value judgments to phenomenological reduction; that is, the phenomenologist did not "experience" these value judgments, but subjected them, as mere facts of consciousness (*Tatsachen des Bewusztseins*), to an exact phenomenological description of their nature. Kant's synthetic *a priori* forms of consciousness were treated in the same manner.

From an unproblematic possession of "sovereign reason," all these forms now became a problematic object of positivistic description that kept strictly to the "facts."

Now modern existentialism tries to surmount this whole positivistic line of thought. It wants to expand philosophy once again into a practical world-view. However, having lost faith in the eternal metaphysical world of ideas that belonged to the humanistic ideal of personality, it no longer strives to regain absolute standards of a supposedly supra-temporal character. In addition, it no longer believes in the possibility of a purely theoretical attitude of thought, in which all preconceptions in one's worldview would be sacrificed to the idea of an absolute theoretical truth.

The old humanistic ideal of science has been undermined. Scientific philosophical thought must arise from the full existence of a person, and must in that sense again become responsible. Human existence, however, is no longer concentrated in a metaphysical center of reason.

Nietzsche admonished humankind: "Brethren, remain true to the earth." His revaluation of all values relativised all eternal values and subordinated them to Superman's brutal historical power-struggle. Kierkegaard, who in mind-set was semi-Christian, posited the notion of an unbridgeable chasm between time and eternity and regarded the human conscience, with its feeling of dread, as the "temporal center of human existence succumbed to time."

Dilthey attempted to infuse the humanistic ideal of personality itself with a historicistic, relativistic content. According to him, the true sovereignty of human personality consists in its ability to free itself from the last remnants of dogmatic confinement by means of genuinely historical thought, and to appropriate for itself the best elements of every phase of culture. However, he exchanged the metaphysical *cogito* (I think), which Descartes regarded as a person's supra-temporal essence, for a dynamic, historically conceived *vivo* (I live). The historical stream of lived experience, which engulfs human existence itself as a fluid element, has usurped the position of the metaphysical focus of thought.

Similarly, Martin Heidegger's ontological philosophy of time sought to disclose the basis of human existence, that of *Dasein* (being), as an immanent historical "being-in-the-world." According to him, human existence is aware of being subject to death; it absorbs this subjection as guilt and in this awareness freely plans its historical future.

This modern existentialist philosophy, weaned from all idealistic Metaphysics and strongly infected by historical relativism, has, like a broad river, engulfed all areas of modern thought. It has become the practical world-view of religiously uprooted modern humankind.

It acknowledges itself as a philosophy of the current spirit of the times, and no longer asks for eternal truth.

It has traded the former rational faith in universally valid laws and norms for a completely irrationalistic faith in the command of the hour (*Gebot der Stunde*), the practical, irreversible demand of the moment.

It has taken on flesh and blood in the irrationalistic view of the state adopted by national socialism and fascism, where the old idealistic ideology represented by the humanistic ideal of personality is replaced by the myths of "the great nation" and of "race and soil." It has replaced the earlier humanistic ideal of science, with its faith in the creative sovereignty of mathematical thought, with a view of science in which theoretical thought is deliberately put at the service of the new world-view. In biology it has introduced an entirely new way of thinking, i.e., that of "holism." In national socialistic and fascist states, it dominates sociology, the science of history, economics, esthetics, legal and political theory, pedagogy, etc. And so the traditional humanistic world-view has fallen into a process of decay and transformation, even though its humanistic root has been maintained.

## A predictable compromise between Christianity and Humanism

It could have been predicted in advance that an intellectually disarmed Christianity would also compromise with this new existentialist philosophy. Under the leadership of Barth and Brunner, "dialectical theology" borrowed its dialectical ground-motive, namely the absolute tension between eternity and time, directly from Sören Kierkegaard's dialectical existential philosophy. From him it also took its notion that the Christian faith has no point of contact with temporal human nature, but can only be understood as a divine leap into a totally different world.

The direct influence of Kierkegaard can also be found in the anthropology of this movement, in particular in its conception of the selfhood as pure actuality, whose being is co-determined by its interpretation of the meaning of existence; and in Brunner's notion of conscience as a knowing feeling of anxiety, the silent groans of a prisoner in his cell, which attest to the inner discord of existence subjected to time, his "sickness unto death."

The whole irrationalistic conception of the evangelical command of love as being a "command of the hour" that transcends every universally valid norm or law, as well as the actualistic conception of the Word of God and of faith as being mere fleeting, "lightning-like" actions of God: these are actually products of the modern philosophy of life, which have now infected the Christian doctrine of faith itself.[1]

In its early days Christian thought already justified its compromises with unbelieving science by means of the scheme of nature and grace. This scheme also adapted itself to modern "dialectical," so called existential thought. The "realm of nature," with its own autonomous ordinances, offers no point of contact for supra-temporal grace. From the very start, the stark dualism between these two was adopted in Kierkegaard's dialectical ground-motive, the absolute tension and contradiction between time and eternity. Karl Barth, for one, carried this dualism to its radical conclusions. In this way, a semi-Christian, dualistic mode of thinking fought the Christian idea of science with all the weapons that unbelieving philosophy had forged against it up to our time.

## A chaos of Protestant attempts at Synthesis

Most Roman Catholics continued to cling to the Aristotelian-Thomistic view of science as the true harmony between "natural" knowledge and "supra-natural knowledge based on divine revelation." Meanwhile, however, the development of Protestant thought presented a chaotic spectacle of attempts at synthesis, from those seeking synthesis with scholasticism and ancient philosophy to those seeking the same with all the evolving variations of humanistic philosophy. In this essay we could only give a bird's eye view of these attempts.

Now the question arises whether the basic idea of the Reformation really could tolerate such a compromise with apostate philosophy. The answer to this question must be an emphatic no! For the Reformation derived its strength precisely from its fundamental break with the dualistic scheme of nature and grace that had always been used to justify syntheses. It returned, at least in the basics, to the Scriptural view that the nature of creation can only be understood in terms of its religious origin, seen through the light of God's Word. That is why it repudiated the Roman Catholic doctrine of grace as a gift which was added to "nature" *(donum superadditum)*. That is why it saw the fall into sin once again, in conformity with Scripture, as a radical corruption of nature that affected

---

1  I have analyzed these issues more extensively in my article: *De Wetsbeschouwing in Brunner's boek "Das Gebot und die Ordnungen,"* (The conception of law in Brunner's work "The Divine Imperative") in the Journal *Antirevolutionaire Staatkunde,* (quarterly organ, published by Kok, Kampen), 1935, pp.1-42.

its religious root. That is also why it rejected the Roman Catholic doctrine of the natural merit of good works and taught justification by faith alone. Finally, that is why it strongly opposed the Roman Catholic view of the temporal institution of the church as the ultimate bond of Christendom. Instead, for its view of human society it once more chose to start with the belief in the religious origin of the human race, reborn in Jesus Christ.

## The Reformational Legacy and its lack of Consistency

It cannot be denied, however, that not all Reformers radically applied this basic Scriptural idea concerning the relationship of the Christian religion to temporal reality in their world-views.

Luther, trained in the nominalist school of Occam ("Ich bin von Occam's Schule'), on the one hand showed the way to the whole Reformation movement after him in his theological understanding of the fall and the redemption. On the other hand in his view of temporal life, he never quite managed to free himself of the late medieval scheme of thought. For him, the law as such was degraded to a rule for sinful life in nature and placed in contrast with the life of grace in evangelical freedom. Therefore, the influence of the nominalist conception on his view of law is clearly seen. Evangelical freedom in Christ Jesus is conceived not merely as a liberation from legalistic servitude, nor merely as a liberation from the curse of the law and a suspension of the ceremonial law of the Jewish "ministry of shadows." Instead, in nominalist fashion, it is seen as the end of subjection to law as such, as life above every rule and universally binding ordinance of God.

Thus, in his world-view, Luther fell back into the nominalistic dualism of nature and grace. Nature, now understood as the realm of temporal ordinances, the "domain of law," was placed in sharp opposition to grace as the realm of evangelical freedom, as living out of evangelical love without law, without subjection to divine rules.

And thus Luther also fell back into the unscriptural notion that the "natural light of reason," common to believers and unbelievers, has the last word in natural, worldly affairs, and that the Christian faith affects only the inner life of the Christian.

It is perfectly true that Luther regarded the philosophy of Aristotle as a great danger for the Christian faith. He spoke out against the acceptance of this philosophy in Protestantism in the most forceful terms. We must not forget, however, that via Aristotelian philosophy Luther wanted to attack the entire Roman Catholic standpoint of synthesis. For he saw very clearly that this philosophy was becoming one of the strongest theoretical mainstays for the entire hierarchical way of thinking in Roman Catholicism.

Luther's standpoint with regard to pagan scholarship remained therefore purely negative. He did not show the way toward a Reformation also of scientific thought in a scriptural, Christian sense. The effects of nominalistic dualism in his view of temporal reality even made that impossible. True, he did see the dangers of the humanistic view of life that was already making forceful advances in his time. His passionate struggle with Erasmus concerning the question of the freedom of the human will became a milestone with respect to the irreconcilable antithesis between Reformation and Humanism which clearly began to emerge. Nevertheless, Luther's academic training was too biased toward late medieval scholasticism for him to have mounted serious attacks on the new humanistic view of science. In Copernicus' new theory of astronomy, which foreboded a radical revolution in the earlier way of scientific thinking, he saw no more than a foolish whim that did not have to be taken seriously.

The task of giving leadership to the Reformation movement in the area of science and university education therefore fell to Philipp Melanchthon, the grandnephew of Johannes Reuchlin. Melanchthon was a man of universal erudition, but he did not have the gift of originality, which must be regarded as essential for accomplishing a real Reformation in this area. Moreover, he was at heart a humanist, and in his youth had been a strong admirer of the great leaders of the humanistic movement: Agricola, Erasmus and Willibald Pirkheimer.

Melanchthon assumed his post at the University of Wittenberg in August 1518 as a twenty-one year old magister. At that time, he gave an address, "Concerning the Reform of the Education of Youth," which was a militant declaration of war against the scholastic "barbarism" that prevailed at the universities. It was imbued with the familiar humanistic arrogance, directed against the mutilation of classical language and philosophy in the era of the "seraphic and cherubic doctors." It was the spirit of Agricola and Erasmus that animated the young Melanchthon. His address had in mind nothing more than the philological, moral and ecclesiastical Reformation favored by these men, that is, a Reformation with a Christian-Stoical hue, but actually in the humanistic, nominalistic spirit.

Melanchthon's electrifying contact with Luther, the hero who was so different from himself in his talents and character, temporarily inspired him with the spirit of reformational antithesis. Between 1519 and 1521, the erstwhile humanist seemed to develop a growing insight into the unbridgeable chasm that divides Christianity from the whole of ancient pagan and scholastic philosophy. In his speech directed against Rhadinus (February 1521), wherein he entered the arena in defense of Martin Luther, and in the *Loci communes rerum theologicarum* (Fundamental Theological Themes, 1521), he rivaled Luther in his sharp condemnation of the "rabulist" (brawling advocate) Aristotle.

On closer scrutiny, however, it was clear that, even in this period, the break with immanence philosophy, which assumes the self-sufficiency of natural reason within its own domain, was not a radical one. Even then, Melanchthon held firmly to the humanistic dialectic. And later when his departure from humanistic ideals had led to a break with his patron Reuchlin, and when Erasmus had turned away from him in disappointment, his old love for Greco-Roman antiquity was rekindled. Then a new phase began in his development which already in 1536 came to a close with his definitive synthesis between Lutheran doctrine of faith and a nominalistic, humanistic interpretation of Aristotelian philosophy.

The whole inner impotence of this Protestant synthesis came to expression in Melanchthon's answer to the question of how one should approach the then current philosophy from the standpoint of the Reformation. "One does best in this regard," he said, "by joining a *respectable school.*"

This answer opened the door for Protestant scholasticism, which soon would make its debut at Protestant universities. It also paved the way for a synthesis in science between the Reformation and Humanism. Protestant thought thereby allowed itself to become ensnared in the basic dilemma of humanistic philosophy and participated in nearly all the evolving variations of the humanistic way of thinking.

Barth and Brunner's most recent attack on the whole idea of Christian science is nothing more than a radical extension of Luther's nominalistic dualism between law and evangelical freedom in synthesis with the modern, equally nominalistic, irrationalistic existentialism. It is merely the old wine of synthesis in new wineskins! And it is Melanchthon's enormous influence that has made possible this whole accommodation between the Reformation and humanistic thought.

Leibniz was the genius of both the German Enlightment and of its bitterest foe, the irrationalistic philosophy of life. He had been educated in the Melanchthon and Aristotelian school of philosophy,[1] and from it he borrowed various motives for his own philosophy. In his thought the scholastic scheme of nature and grace already acquired the content of a

---

1  Cf. E. Weber, *Die philosophische Scholastik des deutschen Protestantismus im Zeitalter der Orthodoxie,* Abhandlugen zur Philosophie und ihrer Geschichte, edited by R. von Falckenberg, 1st Volume, 1907.

synthesis between the humanistic ideals of science and that of personality, between natural necessity and rational freedom.[1] This synthesis was not fruitful at all for the Reformation. The accommodated immanence philosophy, cast in an edifying mold, soon threw off its modest pastoral mask and showed its true face!

## The positive Biblical trend of the Reformation

From the very start, however, there was another current in the great movement of the Reformation. This current sought to take seriously once again the radical significance of the Christian religion for temporal reality. Thus it could not help but bear fruit for the Reformation of scientific thought in the spirit of Scripture.

This current originated neither from Luther nor Melanchthon, nor the Swiss reformer Zwingli, who went even further than Melanchthon in his synthesis between Humanism and the Reformation. Its author rather was John Calvin.

This is not to say that the great reformer of Geneva had already worked out a Christian theory of science. In his youth, Calvin had himself gone through a humanistic phase and was completely familiar with ancient philosophy as well as with the rising Humanism of his own day, both of which he radically rejected. However, he did not develop a philosophy of his own based on the Scriptural, Christian foundations of the Reformation, any more than Luther had done.

Rather, the great significance of the Genevan reformer for the Reformation of scientific thought was that he completely rejected the nominalistic conception of law as well as the dualistic scheme of nature and grace. Of equal significance is that he radically carried through the Augustinian line of thinking, which required that natural knowledge must also be illuminated by God's Word revelation.

Calvin's thought left no room for an autonomous natural reason, because he began once more to take the radical significance of the fall and of redemption in Jesus Christ seriously, also for this life.

Undoubtedly, various remnants of his youthful humanistic phase had stayed with Calvin. The big difference between Calvin and Melanchthon, however, was that the latter deliberately aimed at synthesis, whereas Calvin basically took an antithetic stance, even in his scholarship. He did this without seeking to simply write off the entire development of science in revolutionary fashion, or denying the elements of truth that are found also in apostate thought.

---

1  See my: *De Wijsbegeerte der Wetsidee*, Bk.I (Amsterdam, Paris, 1935), Part II, pp.181 ff. (*A New Critique of Theoretical Thought*, Vol.I, pp.150 ff.).

If this Scriptural direction of thinking had been able to permeate the Protestant universities, Christian scientific thought would certainly have developed in a very different manner. It was not Calvin, however, but Melanchthon who set the course in this area for the next few centuries.

As a result the development of modern science ultimately bypassed the Reformation and fell completely under humanistic leadership.

The Protestant attempts at synthesis even lacked completely the undeniably grand design of Thomism. For they were rooted in a nominalistic dualism that left no room for a real synthesis between natural knowledge and the Christian faith. At best they could only strive for an external religious truce between the two. That is why the Kantian dualism between science and faith had such enormous popularity among Protestant advocates of synthesis.

The intellectual disarmament of Christianity in the field of science therefore inevitably assumed much more radical forms in later Protestant thought than it did in Roman Catholic thought. For in Roman Catholic circles, ecclesiastical leadership could always still impose a final restraint, albeit from the outside, on the process of deformation, and by its authority it could ensure the Thomistic view of science of a dominant and cohesive position.

## Integral Christian Scholarship requires the Foundation of a Biblically informed Philosophy

At first, therefore, the idea of a radically Christian science appeared to have lost its case. Nevertheless, it was an idea that could not be eradicated. Sometime or other, eyes had to open to the fact that the very alliance with the humanistic idea of science had inflicted untold damage on the cause of the Reformation.

Toward the end of the nineteenth century, the Calvinistic revival in the Netherlands ushered in a potent new development in the Scriptural view of science.

In this regard, Dr. Kuyper's proclamation that the antithesis holds sway also in the domain of science and the founding of the Free University as a consequence of this, must be viewed as a turning point of the utmost significance. The proponents of dialectical theology keenly perceived that this Calvinistic movement was their most serious adversary, also in the area of science. For indeed, Kuyper's antithetic viewpoint in science, a viewpoint that was misinterpreted in a very narrow-minded way, is incompatible with the notion, advocated by Barth and Brunner, that the Christian religion is materially irrelevant for a scientific investigation of the structure of temporal reality.

Over against the password of intellectual disarmament in science, Kuyper posed the scriptural demand that Christianity should be allowed to participate, fully armed, in the development of science. He rejected the autonomy of natural reason fundamentally and on every front.

Will this scriptural point of view be carried through further in scientific thought, or will the striving for synthesis once more gain the upper hand over the antithetic course in science as charted by Kuyper? That is the big question for the future of reformational Christian thought.

*One* thing is certain: genuinely Christian scholarship can no longer do without the foundation of a scriptural philosophy.

I have pointed out earlier that, in modern times, the intellectual disarmament of Christianity in scholarship has been promoted in great measure by the unquestioned acceptance of the modern humanistic line of demarcation between the special sciences and philosophy. The positivistic trend of thought in the special sciences wishes to confront Christian thought with a *fait accompli*. This school is so dangerous, precisely because it has clothed the idea of neutrality in science in the deceptive garb of evidence. After all, what could be more independent of the Christian religion than the investigation of objective facts? Here is where Scriptural philosophy must intervene in order to open the eyes of the Christian researcher to the uncritical and misleading character of this positivistic attitude of thought.

For the "facts" cannot be grasped scientifically without insight into their structure, which is determined by the divine world-order. And insight into this structure depends absolutely on the question of where the thinker chooses his or her starting-point. Meaning is the mode of being of all created reality, and meaning does not repose within itself, but points restlessly above and beyond itself to the Origin of all things.

This state of affairs makes a separation between the special sciences and philosophy impossible.

We have observed in the foregoing why the humanistic idea of science is incompatible with the acceptance of a divine world-order which controls the mutual relationship and coherence of the distinct aspects of temporal reality and has its deeper root-unity in the religious center of human existence. We have seen how this humanistic idea, due to its failure to recognize the true root of temporal reality, tried time and again to level the structures that God ordained in His creation.

Actually, no special science is possible without making an implicit epistemic choice in respect of the mutual relationship and coherence of the various aspects of reality chosen by theoretical thought for its field of study.

Mathematics already presupposes a philosophical idea regarding the mutual relations of number, space, movement and logical thought. Depending on how this idea is conceived, mathematical researchers part company in several different directions (formalism, logicism, intuitionism, empiricism). And these differences in philosophical insight do not have merely speculative significance; they intervene squarely within mathematical research itself. This can be seen clearly enough in the fact that the intuitionistic school, for example, rejects the validity of entire sections of so-called higher mathematics erected by formalism and logicism, and that it demands an entirely new design for it.

In physics, modern development since Planck, Schrödinger and Heisenberg has unleashed a fundamental controversy about the problem of causality.

In modern biology, the mechanistic, neo-vitalistic and holistic movements regard each other as fierce adversaries. Psychology is a veritable hotbed of contending schools. Even in logic, there is an all-out struggle between different philosophical schools. Just consider the contrast between the older Aristotelian logic of inclusion and the modern logic of relations (symbolic logic), or that between the psychologistic school and the modern school of "pure logic."

The idea that the science of history could be a safe haven for the positivistic mind can only be entertained by one who is still caught up in the naive prejudice that historical facts can be known apart from an insight into the meaning of their structure and their coherence. Even the positivistic conception of history, which dissolves all of human society into a complex of purely historical phenomena, is essentially oriented to a historicistic philosophical perspective on the coherence of the various aspects of reality.

The conception which denies that historical phenomena are governed by any kind of law is equally rooted in a nominalistic, historicistic view of history. Or does one think that the historian can investigate, for example, whether during the Middle Ages there was still such a thing as public law, without a subjective insight into the structure of the state? And does one then accept as philosophically unbiased the historicistic viewpoint that the science of history alone can disclose to us the nature of the state?

Consider further the separation between ethnology and the science of history, the question whether or not history has a normative meaning, or the meaning of the concept of historical causality. These are all philosophical questions, which take on special scientific significance as soon as one begins to interpret the factual material one has assembled.

Need I refer also to linguistics, sociology, economics, jurisprudence, moral theory and theology? In each of these special sciences, the conflict between the various schools of thought shows itself to be of an essentially philosophical nature.

Enough! The prejudice of the positivistic attitude believed it could remove these sciences from the conflict between philosophical viewpoints by holding them rigorously to the examination of "objective facts." But the biased nature of that attitude in recent times has already been exposed from such widely divergent angles that naive positivism in the special sciences can only be called uncritical and unscientific.

One must never forget that the positivistic attitude in the special sciences is rooted in a positivistic philosophical perspective on the structure of experience and reality. Of the abundance of God's creation, this philosophical point of view has left us with nothing but a naturalistic abstraction, which in turn is itself merely the product of theoretical philosophical thinking which has declared itself autonomous.

Let no Christian thinker continue in the belief that when working in any special science he or she can accept this positivistic view of reality without denying his or her Christian faith.

By means of the traditional scheme of nature and grace, Christian thought sought for centuries to justify either a divorce between faith and science or a compromise between Christian faith and pagan philosophy. But, precisely if used in that way, this scheme is inherently false, because it is itself in conflict with the structure of our temporal existence as determined by the divine world-order.

By virtue of this structural law, our cognitive function is necessarily guided by the function of faith, even though these two functions are mutually irreducible and each of them is enclosed within its own lawsphere. All believing is a reaching out with the faith function of our existence to the ultimate, eternal basis of Truth and certainty to which the laws of our scientific thought themselves refer. All faith and belief are bound to divine revelation.

Now, the Lord God has revealed Himself throughout His entire creation, and centrally in the human heart, the root of human existence. From the very beginning, clarity of this revelation of God in the "nature" of creation needed to be obtained through the divine Word-revelation, which required listening with a believing heart to God's Word.

Humankind's fall into sin, which also necessarily distracted its thought from the Truth, resulted in the *closing of its heart to the divine Word-revelation, no longer listening to God's Word.* With this, of course, the natural faith function of a person's temporal life did not cease to exist, but it was pointed in an apostate direction. Faith, having become apostate, began to look for God and human selfhood in the temporal world. Egotistically it began to *design* its own gods from "God's revelation in nature," which no longer was clarified by the Word of God. This is also how faith in the self-sufficiency and the creative character of science was born, as *idolatry* in the true sense of the word.

Every act of declaring certain aspects or structures of reality self-sufficient, every attempt to make them stand on their own, fundamentally proceeds from a deification of the theoretical thought that carries out such acts of isolation and abstraction.

It is an apostate faith that manifests itself in the proclamation of the religious neutrality of human thought. This apostate faith inevitably results in pulling thought away from the fullness of Truth and leads it down false paths.

God's common grace does not mean that this apostasy has no factual influence in science. It means only that in Christ Jesus, God continues to maintain His world-order, the structure of His creation, and thus also the structure of our cognitive function. It means that He distributes His individual gifts, also in the domain of science, to believers and unbelievers alike.

Whoever seeks to exclude Christ Jesus as the Fullness of Divine Revelation from the domain of science, however, misuses God's gift and *stands outside of the Truth, even in the way he or she thinks.* That person does remain bound to the universally valid laws of human experience and, when staying in touch with reality, can make important contributions to the development of scientific knowledge. Nevertheless, making theoretical thought self-sufficient always leads to an obscuring of insight into the structure of reality. Certain modal aspects or individuality structures of the facts under examination are absolutized at the expense of others and are torn theoretically from their coherence in the cosmos. Precisely for this reason, apostate science lacks a focus on the Truth and of necessity must time and again lead to a distorted interpretation of the states of affairs it discovers.

Science, moreover, is not a task of isolated individuals but a communal enterprise. Under the leadership of those who are especially gifted, many people cooperate in order to increase a store of knowledge that has been amassed over many generations. Every scientist, in turn, must draw from this store for his or her own work.

Furthermore, in accordance with the divine world-order itself, science operates in history under the guidance of a cultural spirit, which in its turn is ultimately guided by a faith.

Modern science is undeniably pervaded by the cultural spirit and the faith of Western Humanism. Because of this, throughout the whole course of its development, it is rooted in the idea of the autonomy, or rather the self-sufficiency, of scientific thought.

This confronts those Christian scientists and scholars who want to take the Christian view of science seriously (in radical fashion) with a seemingly hopeless task. They too have to draw from a common store of knowledge, and must cooperate in the communal task of further developing human knowledge.

They cannot stand aloof from the scientific community as isolated individuals. Nevertheless, they cannot accept the actual course of development that science has taken as a "fait accompli." Instead, they have the calling to subject this course of development to the constant critique of the Scriptural idea of Christian science and scholarship. This idea does not consist of an external accommodation of the results of science to the Christian faith. Rather, it means an internal transformation of the theoretical view of the structure of reality and of human experience, so that both can once more be seen from the perspective of their true center and Origin.

This is not an attempt at arrogant dismantlement, which is doomed to futility from the start. What is at stake, in the full sense of the word, is a Reformation of scientific thought in a Scriptural, Christian sense.

In order to accomplish that, however, a tremendous historical and cultural battle has to be fought against a humanistic spirit in the sciences, a spirit that seeks to exclude from the scientific community all who stand in its way.

For Humanism has indeed managed to acquire the historical power to shape scientific development, thanks to a centuries-long attempt at synthesis on the part of Christian thought itself.

All Christians who in their scientific work are ashamed of the Name of Christ Jesus, because they desire honor among people, will be totally useless in the mighty struggle to recapture science, one of the great powers of Western culture, for the Kingdom of God. This struggle is not hopeless, however, so long as it is waged in the full armour of faith in Him who has said "All authority in heaven and on earth has been given to Me," and again, "Take heart! I have overcome the world."

# Herman Dooyeweerd – A Biographical Sketch[1]

Mr. President, Members of the Board, Faculty, Staff and Students, Distinguished Guests, Ladies and Gentlemen:

Many of you will be very familiar with the work of the late Herman Dooyeweerd, who he was, what he stood for, what he wrote and what impact he had in his own country and in other places around the world.

On the other hand, I suspect there are quite a few others here tonight who know little more about Dooyeweerd than his name, the fact that he lived in Holland, that he was involved in the development of a rather complex sounding philosophy which is called the "Philosophy of the Cosmonomic Idea" and that it is variously referred to as a "Calvinist" philosophy or as a "Christian" philosophy.

Those in our audience who belong to the second group may well be asking themselves a number of questions. For instance, who was this man, what did he actually do, why is he apparently considered so important that there should be an academic centre named after him in North America; what is the centre meant to accomplish and why is it at Redeemer College? Also, what is the "Dooyeweerd Foundation" and what is its role in all this?

This evening's other speakers will address most of these questions. However, to provide at least some minimal background for those who are not well acquainted with Dooyeweerd's work, I thought that, before we get too much further into this evening, it might be helpful if I used the time at my disposal to provide a brief biographical sketch of Dooyeweerd as seen from my personal perspective as his eldest son.

Herman Dooyeweerd was a Dutch philosopher who achieved international stature. He is considered by many one of the foremost philosophers – some think *the* foremost – The Netherlands has produced from a long line of eminent thinkers going back some three hundred years and including names such as Erasmus and Spinoza. Both the Encyclopaedia Britannica and the Italian Encyclopaedia Filosofica have sections con-

---

1 Remarks by Herman Dooyeweerd Jr., President of *The Herman Dooyeweerd Foundation*, delivered on the occasion of the official opening of "The Dooyeweerd Centre for Christian Philosophy" at Redeemer College, on November 5, 1994.

taining references to Dooyeweerd's philosophical thought. Some of his writings have already been translated and published in English. Several were originally written in French or in German by Dooyeweerd himself, while still others were translated after his death into Korean, Japanese and Spanish. Just last month I received in the mail from Italy a brand new publication representing a translation, from French into Italian, of a series of five lectures Dooyeweerd gave in France in the 1950's. So we are beginning to see translations of translations.

Dooyeweerd's work is considered to be a major contribution toward the development of a new Christian systematic philosophy that in its scope, its thoroughly scholarly approach and depth of its philosophical insight and reasoning need in no way take a backseat to other more widely known and academically acclaimed philosophies.

Yet Dooyeweerd did not set out to be a philosopher. He was born in Amsterdam 100 years ago last month. He was raised in a staunchly Calvinist family. His father was a bookkeeper with the Dutch Department of Taxation and a private tax consultant in his spare time. He was well read, had a great respect for scholarly work, had a deep affinity for the arts, especially poetry, and was a devoted follower of the renowned preacher, writer and statesman, Dr. Abraham Kuyper, and the christian renewal movement he had founded. All these values, including many of those so eloquently articulated by Dr. Kuyper, he passed on to his son and to his other children who greatly loved and respected him.

The young Dooyeweerd received a classical high school education at a christian school a stone's throw from the Free University.

Although his mother had encouraged him to become a stockbroker, Dooyeweerd was not attracted to that idea. Instead, he wanted to study but wasn't sure what exactly. He was deeply impressed with literature but in the end he settled for law.

He enrolled at the Free University, which had been established in 1880 by Dr. Kuyper and others as a reformed Christian university. There Dooyeweerd obtained a Ph.D. in law at the young age of 22. His thesis was entitled "The Cabinet Ministers under Dutch Constitutional Law." It was very favourably reviewed in the press at the time and remains a standard reference work to this day.

Dooyeweerd's first job was as an assistant tax inspector in the Province of Friesland, followed by a one-year stint as assistant to a municipal councillor in the old university city of Leiden. Less than a year later he was asked to join the national government's Ministry of Labour where he became deputy head of the Public Health Department in The Hague.

During his few years in government service Dooyeweerd spent much of his free time furthering his studies at home, particularly in legal philosophy. Time and again, he found a lot of divergence, if not confusion, amongst legal philosophers with each advocating a different and often conflicting philosophical approach to law, none of which he was able to reconcile with his own deeply-felt religious beliefs.

This convinced Dooyeweerd that there was a great need for a more deeply thought-out comprehensive philosophy which would give a more credible account of the world in which we live and the structures and interaction of the various aspects of what we feel, see and experience around us. Above all, it should provide a genuinely christian and biblically based insight and foundation.

In 1922, Dooyeweerd got his chance to develop his philosophical thought in earnest and to apply it in a very practical sense. At the time, the political party Dr. Kuyper had founded and led from its inception was one of the leading government parties. Not long after Dr. Kuyper's death, the three men who had inherited the leadership of the party saw the need for the creation of a new academic research institute – or "think tank" in today's vernacular – to advise the party on foundational matters that should govern future policy proposals advanced by the party.

Dooyeweerd, at age 27, was identified and picked over six much older candidates by the then Minister of Defence and by the Prime Minister – both also representing the senior leadership of the party – to become the first director of the party's new research institute. In accepting this post, Dooyeweerd had insisted that he be given sufficient time to develop the sound philosophical foundations he believed should govern any Christian party and the state, society at large as well as its individual citizens.

It was during his five years at this research institute – still in existence today and known as the Kuyper Institute – that his philosophical ideas began to take definitive shape.

He was to make his final career move five years later when, at the age of only 32, he accepted an offer to become professor at the Free University, not in philosophy but in the faculty of law. There he remained for the next 40 years teaching *Encyclopedia of Law*, *Old Dutch Law* and *Dutch Constitutional Law* until his retirement in 1965 at the age of 70.

His years at the Free University were eventful ones. It was there in the 1930's, during the Great Depression, that he completed his most prominent work, his *magnum opus* consisting of more than 2200 pages, setting out his systematic philosophy. In 1953 an English edition was published in North America containing extensive revisions and additions reflecting the further development of his thought during the intervening years. This period, of course, included the five long and dark years of the Second World War and the occupation and brutal suppression of Holland by the Nazis.

When the War had ended and all public energy and attention was focused on reconstruction and rebuilding of society and its political and other institutions, Dooyeweerd took a very active part in the debates that took place to accomplish those objectives. He used his position as chief editor of a weekly newspaper to make his views known.

For more than 30 years he was also chief editor of an international periodical for reformed christian philosophy, a publication of the Association of Reformational Philosophy which Dooyeweerd and his brother-in-law, Professor Vollenhoven, founded in the mid-1930s and which today has a membership of several hundred people in more than a dozen countries. He contributed numerous articles and editorials of his own in addition to editing other people's contributions and doing new book reviews. In all, including several major works, his writings comprise over 200 titles.

Now, to round out the picture, a few comments on Dooyeweerd's personal life:

☐ He was, as they say, "happily married." His wife was a lovely and remarkable lady (this is not just on my say-so because I could of course be biased!). They had nine children. To his regret, none went to university, let alone followed even remotely in his footsteps.

☐ He loved art, especially music and poetry. He was an accomplished recreational pianist and played daily on the grand piano in his study. His favourites were Chopin and Tchaikowsky. He also liked to improvise on his own.

☐ He liked detective stories and was often seen to slip away from a birthday party or other gathering at home to go upstairs to listen to the radio when his favourite mystery or detective program was coming on.

☐ He became a rather avid soccer fan, first via the radio, later also via t.v., especially when the famous Ajax team in Amsterdam was playing.

☐ He could enjoy a little jazz and did not seem to mind when in later years his youngest son, who is a professional jazz musician (bass and composition) seemed more readily identified by the public with the name Dooyeweerd than he was himself.

☐ He faithfully did an hour's strenuous exercise every morning, even on his travels.

☐ He had an immense personal professional library at home which occupied every wall, floor to ceiling, in the two large rooms which made up his study, spilling over in the same fashion into the hallways of the same floor and the one above it. He claimed to have read each and every volume. There was no reason to doubt him because he always seemed to know exactly where to look for a specific quotation from a particular book.

☐ He was a deeply religious person and a faithful church goer. However, his regular church attendance did not prevent him from the occasional strong criticism of a particular minister or his sermon when he arrived home after the service.

☐ He was active in numerous organizations, including the *Juliana Hospital* in Amsterdam and a Prisons and Prisoners Rehabilitation organization which is more or less the Dutch equivalent of the *John Howard Society.* He was the chairman of the boards of both for many years.

I hope that my comments so far helped to give you an idea of some of Dooyeweerd's accomplishments and some of the personal aspects of his life.

However, I should mention one more thing and that is his foreign travels which took him on lecture tours to Switserland, South Africa, France, the U.S.A. and Canada. His North American tour in particular was long and very arduous. Accompanied by his wife, he was underway for many months and spoke at numerous major and other universities and colleges from coast to coast in both the U.S.A. and Canada. The lectures and innumerable smaller events and social gatherings created a following of people on this continent. Many of them still recall from time to time that first encounter with Dooyeweerd, who was by all accounts a dynamic speaker.

The trip, while a success in many respects, took a heavy physical toll from which he really never fully recovered. The premature death of his wife also affected him deeply.

From my rather long "thumbnail sketch" you may feel that I have been engaged in putting Dooyeweerd on somewhat of a "pedestal". If that was so, my father would have strongly disapproved. Instead, I hope I have succeeded in showing that Dooyeweerd was a gifted man but in many ways also a very down-to-earth person with his feet firmly on the ground. We in the family loved him dearly and are, we think justifiably, proud of him. We remember him as someone who was humble before God and always strove to be in his service. In the days just before his death I personally witnessed how he struggled greatly with the fact that in his own eyes he had not done all that he had seemingly felt God had called him to do.

Now, before I conclude my remarks, I would like to take this opportunity, speaking as President of The Herman Dooyeweerd Foundation and on behalf of the Dooyeweerd family, to hereby publicly express my appreciation to Redeemer College, especially its new President, Dr. Justin Cooper, its former President, Reverend Henry De Bolster, members of the Board, members and past members of the Steering Committee and the faculty and staff who all helped make the "Dooyeweerd Centre for Christian Philosophy" become a reality.

Thank you.

# Glossary

[The following glossary of Dooyeweerd's technical terms and neologisms is reproduced and edited by Daniël F. M. Strauss, with the permission of its author, Albert M. Wolters, from C. T. McIntire, ed., *The Legacy of Herman Dooyeweerd: Reflections on Critical Philosophy in the Christian Tradition* (Lanham MD, 1985), pp. 167-171.]

THIS GLOSSARY OF HERMAN DOOYEWEERD'S terms is an adapted version of the one published in L. Kalsbeek, *Contours of a Christian Philosophy* (Toronto: Wedge, 1975). It does not provide exhaustive technical definitions but gives hints and pointers for a better understanding. Entries marked with an asterisk are those terms which are used by Dooyeweerd in a way which is unusual in English-speaking philosophical contexts and are, therefore, a potential source of misunderstanding. Words or phrases in small caps and beginning with a capital letter refer to other entries in this glossary.

* **Analogy** (see LAW-SPHERE) – Collective name for a RETROCIPATION or an ANTICIPATION.

* **Anticipation** – An ANALOGY within one MODALITY referring to a later modality. An example is "efficiency," a meaning-moment which is found within the historical modality, but which points forward to the later economic modality. Contrast with RETROCIPATION.

* **Antinomy** – Literally "conflict of laws" (from Greek *anti*, "against," and *nomos*, "law"). A logical contradiction arising out of a failure to distinguish the different kinds of law valid in different MODALITIES. Since ontic laws do not conflict (Principium Exclusae Antinomiae), an antinomy is always a logical sign of ontological reductionism.

* **Antithesis** – Used by Dooyeweerd (following Abraham Kuyper) in a specifically religious sense to refer to the fundamental spiritual opposition between the kingdom of God and the kingdom of darkness. See Galatians 5:17. Since this is an opposition between regimes, not realms, it runs through every department of human life and culture, including philosophy and the academic enterprise as a whole, and through the heart of every believer as he or she struggles to live a life of undivided allegiance to God.

111

**Aspect** – A synonym for MODALITY.

**Cosmonomic idea** – Dooyeweerd's own English rendering of the Dutch term *wetsidee*. Occasionally equivalents are "transcendental ground idea" or "transcendental basic idea". The intention of this new term is to bring to expression that there exists an unbreakable coherence between God's *law* (nomos) and created reality (*cosmos*) factually subjected to God's law.

**Dialectic** – In Dooyeweerd's usage: an unresolvable tension, within a system or line of thought, between two logically irreconcilable polar positions. Such a dialectical tension is characteristic of each of the three non-Christian GROUND-MOTIVES which Dooyeweerd sees as having dominated Western thought.

**\*Enkapsis (enkaptic)** – A neologism borrowed by Dooyeweerd from the Swiss biologist Heidenhain, and derived from the Greek *enkaptein, "to swallow up."* The term refers to the structural interlacements which can exist between things, plants, animals, and societal structures which have their own internal structural principle and independent qualifying function. As such, enkapsis is to be clearly distinguished from the part-whole relation, in which there is a common internal structure and qualifying function.

**Factual Side** – General designation of whatever is *subjected* to the LAW-SIDE of creation (see SUBJECT-SIDE).

**Founding function** – The earliest of the two modalities which characterize certain types of structural wholes. The other is called the GUIDING FUNCTION. For example, the founding function of the family is the biotic modality.

**\* Gegenstand** – A German word for "object," used by Dooyeweerd as a technical term for a modality when abstracted from the coherence of time and opposed to the analytical function in the theoretical attitude of thought, thereby establishing the Gegenstand relation. Gegenstand is therefore the technically precise word for the object of SCIENCE, while "object" itself is reserved for the objects of NAIVE EXPERIENCE.

**Ground-motive** – The Dutch term *grondmotief*, used by Dooyeweerd in the sense of fundamental motivation, driving force. He distinguished four basic ground-motives in the history of Western civilization:
(1) form and matter, which dominated pagan Greek philosophy; (2) nature and grace, which underlay medieval Christian synthesis thought (3) nature and freedom, which has shaped the philosophies of modern times; and (4) creation, fall, and redemption, which lies at the root of a radical and integrally scriptural philosophy.

**Guiding function** – The highest subject function of a structural whole (e.g. stone, animal, business enterprise, or state). Except in the case of humans, this function is also said to QUALIFY the structural whole. It is called the guiding function because it "guides" or "leads" its earlier functions. For example, the guiding function of a plant is the biotic. The physical function of a plant (as studied, e.g. by biochemistry) is different from physical functioning elsewhere because of its being "guided" by the biotic. Also called "leading function".

* **Heart** – The concentration point of human existence; the supratemporal focus of all human temporal functions; the religious root unity of humans. Dooyeweerd says that it was his rediscovery of the biblical idea of the heart as the central religious depth dimension of human multifaceted life which enabled him to wrestle free from neo-Kantianism and phenomenology. The Scriptures speak of this focal point also as "soul," "spirit," and "inner man." Philiosophical equivalents are Ego, I, I-ness, and Selfhood. It is the heart in this sense which survives death, and it is by the religious redirection of the heart in regeneration that all human temporal functions are renewed.

* **Immanence Philosophy** – A name for all non-Christian philosophy, which tries to find the ground and integration of reality *within* the created order. Unlike Christianity, which acknowledges a transcendent Creator above all things, immanence philosophy of necessity absolutizes some feature or aspect of creation itself.

* **Individuality-structure** – This term represents arguably one of the most difficult concepts in Dooyeweerd's philosophy. Coined in both Dutch and English by Dooyeweerd himself it has led sometimes to serious misunderstandings amongst scholars. Over the years there have been various attempts to come up with an alternate term, some of which are described below, but in the absence of a consensus it was decided to leave the term the way it is.

It is the general name or the characteristic law (order) of concrete things, as given by virtue of creation. Individuality-structures belong to the law-side of reality. Dooyeweerd uses the term individuality-structure to indicate the applicability of a structural order *for* the existence of *individual* entities. Thus the *structural laws* for the state, for marriage, for works of art, for mosquitoes, for sodium chloride, and so forth are called individuality-structures. The idea of an individual whole is determined by an individuality-structure which precedes the theoretical analysis of its modal functions. The identity of an individual whole is a relative unity in a multiplicity of functions. (See MODALITY.) Van Riessen prefers to call this law for entities an *identity-structure*, since as such it guarantees the persistent **identity** of all entities (*Wijsbegeerte*, Kampen 1970, p.158). In his work (*Alive, An Enquiry into the Origin and Meaning of Life*, 1984, Ross House Books, Vallecito, California), M. Verbrugge introduces his own distinct systematic account concerning the nature of (what he calls) *functors*, a word first introduced by Hendrik Hart for the dimension of individuality-structures (cf. Hart: *Understanding Our World, Towards an Integral Ontology*, New York 1984, cf.pp.445-446). As a substitute for the notion of an individuality-structure, Verbrugge advances the term: *idionomy* (cf. *Alive*, pp.42, 81ff., 91ff.). Of course this term may also cause misunderstanding if it is taken to mean that each individual creature (subject) has its *own unique* law. What is intended is that every *type of law* (*nomos*) is meant to delimit and determine unique subjects. In other words, however *specified* the universality of the law may be, it can never, in its bearing upon unique individual creatures, itself become something *uniquely individual*. Another way of grasping the meaning of Dooyeweerd's notion of an *individuality-structure* is, in following an oral suggestion by Roy Clouser (Zeist, August 1986), to call it a *type-law* (from Greek: *typonomy*). This simply means that all entities of a certain *type* conform to this law. The following perspective given by M.D. Stafleu elucidates this terminology in a *systematic way* (*Time and Again, A Systematic Analysis of the Foundations of Physics*, Wedge Publishing Foundation, Toronto 1980, p.6, 11): *typical laws* (type-laws/typonomies, such as the Coulomb law – applicable only to charged entities and the Pauli principle – applicable only to fermions) are special laws which apply to a limited class of entities only, whereas *modal laws* hold universally for all possible entities. D.F.M. Strauss ('*Inleiding tot die Kosmologie*', SACUM, Bloemfontein 1980) introduces the expression *entity structures*. The term **entity** comprises both the *individuality* and the *identity* of the thing concerned – therefore it accounts for the respective emphases found in Dooyeweerd's notion of *individuality-structures* and in Van Riessen's notion of *identity structures*. The following words of Dooyeweerd show that both the **individuality** and **identity** of an entity is determined by its 'individuality-structure': "In general we can establish that the factual temporal duration of a thing as an individual and identical whole is dependent on the preservation of its structure of individuality" (*A New Critique of Theoretical Thought*, Vol.III:79).

**Irreducibility (irreducible)** – Incapability of theoretical reduction. This is the negative way of referring to the unique distinctiveness of things and aspects which we find everywhere in creation and which theoretical thought must respect. Insofar as everything has its own peculiar created nature and character, it cannot be understood in terms of categories foreign to itself.

**\* Law** – The notion of creational law is central to Dooyeweerd's philosophy. Everything in creation is subject to God's law for it, and accordingly law is the boundary between God and creation. Scriptural synonyms for law are "ordinance," "decree," "commandment," "word," and so on. Dooyeweerd stresses that law is not in opposition to but the condition for true freedom. See also NORM and LAW-SIDE.

**Law-Side** – The created cosmos, for Dooyeweerd, has two correlative "sides": a law-side and a factual side (initially called: SUBJECT-SIDE). The former is simply the coherence of God's laws or ordinances for creation; the latter is the totality of created reality which is subject to those laws. It is important to note that the law-side always holds universally.

**Law-Sphere** (see MODAL STRUCTURE and MODALITY) – The circle of laws qualified by a unique, irreducible and indefinable meaning-nucleus is known as a law-sphere. Within every law-sphere temporal reality has a modal function and in this function is subjected (French: *sujet*) to the laws of the modal spheres. Therefore every law-sphere has a law-side and a subject-side that are given only in unbreakable correlation with each other. (See DIAGRAM on p.119.)

**\* Meaning** – Dooyeweerd uses the word "meaning" in an unusual sense. By it he means the referential, non-self-sufficient character of created reality in that it points beyond itself to God as Origin. Dooyeweerd stresses that reality *is* meaning in this sense and that, therefore, it does not *have* meaning. "Meaning" is the Christian alternative to the metaphysical substance of immanence philosphy. "Meaning" becomes almost a synonym for "reality." Note the many compounds formed from it: meaning-nucleus, meaning-side, meaning-moment, meaning-fullness.

**\* Meaning-nucleus** – The indefinable core meaning of a MODALITY.

**Modality** (See MODAL STRUCTURE and LAW-SPHERE) – One of the fifteen fundamental ways of being distinguished by Dooyeweerd. As modes of being, they are sharply distinguished from the concrete things which function within them. Initially Dooyeweerd distinguished fourteen aspects only, but since 1950 he introduced the kinematical aspect of *uniform movement* between the spatial and the physical aspects. Modalities are also known as "modal functions," "modal aspects," or as "facets" of created reality. (See DIAGRAM on p.119.)

**Modal Structure** (see MODALITY and LAW-SPHERE) – The peculiar constellation, in any given modality, of its meaning-moments (anticipatory, retrocipatory, nuclear). Contrast INDIVIDUALITY-STRUCTURE.

**\* Naive experience** – Human experience insofar as it is not "theoretical" in Dooyeweerd's precise sense. "Naive" does not mean unsophisticated. Sometimes called "ordinary" or "everyday" experience. Dooyeweerd takes pains to emphasize that theory is embedded in this everyday experience and must not violate it.

**Norm (normative)** – Postpsychical laws, that is, modal laws for the analytical through pistical law-spheres (see LAW-SPHERE and DIAGRAM on p.119). These laws are norms because they need to be positivized (see POSITIVIZE) and can be violated, in distinction from the "natural laws" of the pre-analytical spheres which are obeyed involuntarily (e.g., in a digestive process).

**\* Nuclear-moment** – A synonym for MEANING-NUCLEUS and LAW-SPHERE, used to designate the indefinable core meaning of a MODALITY or aspect of created reality.

**\* Object** – Something qualified by an object function and thus correlated to a subject function. A work of art, for instance, is qualified by its correlation to the human subjective function of aesthetic appreciation. Similarly, the elements of a sacrament are pistical objects.

**Opening process** – The process by which latent modal anticipations are "opened" or actualized. The modal meaning is then said to be "deepened." It is this process which makes possible the cultural development (differentiation) of society from a primitive ("closed," undifferentiated) stage. For example, by the opening or disclosure of the ethical anticipation in the juridical aspect, the modal meaning of the legal aspect is deepened and society can move from the principle of "an eye for an eye" to the consideration of extenuating circumstances in the administration of justice.

**\* Philosophy** – In Dooyeweerd's precise systematic terminology, philosophy is the encyclopedic science, that is, its proper task is the theoretical investigation of the overall systematic integration of the various scientific disciplines and their fields of inquiry. Dooyeweerd also uses the term in a more inclusive sense, especially when he points out that all philosophy is rooted in a pretheoretical religious commitment and that some philosophical conception, in turn, lies at the root of all scientific scholarship.

**Positivize** – A word coined to translate the Dutch word *positiveren*, which means to make positive in the sense of being actually valid in a given time or place. For example, positive law is the legislation which is in force in a given country at a particular time; it is contrasted with the *legal principles* which lawmakers must positivize as legislation. In a general sense, it refers to the responsible implementation of all normative principles in human life as embodied, for example, in state legislation, economic policy, ethical guidelines, and so on.

**Qualify** – The GUIDING FUNCTION of a thing is said to qualify it in the sense of characterizing it. In this sense a plant is said to be qualified by the biotic and a state by the juridical [aspects].

**\* Radical** – Dooyeweerd frequently uses this term with an implicit reference to the Greek meaning of *radix* = *root*. This usage must not be confused with the political connotation of the term *radical* in English. In other works Dooyeweerd sometimes paraphrases his use of the term radical with the phrase: *penetrating to the root of created reality*.

**\* Religion (religious)** – For Dooyeweerd, religion is not an area or sphere of life but the all-encompassing and direction-giving root of it. It is service of

God (or a substitute no-god) in every domain of human endeavor. As such, it is to be sharply distinguished from religious faith, which is but one of the many acts and attitudes of human existence. Religion is an affair of the HEART and so directs all human functions. Dooyeweerd says religion is "the innate impulse of the human selfhood to direct itself toward the *true* or toward a *pretended* absolute Origin of all temporal diversity of meaning" (*A New Critique of Theoretical Thought*, Vol.I, 1953, p.57).

* **Retrocipation** – A feature in one MODALITY which refers to, is reminiscent of, an earlier one, yet retaining the modal qualification of the aspect in which it is found. The "extension" of a concept, for example, is a kind of logical space: it is a strictly logical affair, and yet it harks back to the spatial modality in its original sense. See ANTICIPATION.

* **Science** – Two things are noted about Dooyeweerd's use of the term "science". In the first place, as a translation of the Dutch word *wetenschap* (analogous to the German word Wissenschaft), it embraces all scholarly study – not only the natural sciences but also the social sciences and the humanities, including theology and philosophy. In the second place, science is always, strictly speaking, a matter of modal abstraction, that is, of analytically lifting an aspect out of the temporal coherence in which it is found and examining it in the Gegenstand relation. But in this investigation it does not focus its theoretical attention upon the modal structure of such an aspect itself; rather, it focuses on the coherence of the actual phenomena which function within that structure. Modal abstraction as such must be distinguished from NAIVE EXPERIENCE. In the first sense, therefore, "science" has a wider application in Dooyeweerd than is usual in English-speaking countries, but in the second sense it has a more restricted, technical meaning.

**Sphere Sovereignty** – A translation of Kuyper's phrase *souvereiniteit in eigen kring*, by which he meant that the various distinct spheres of human authority (such as family, church, school, and business enterprise) each have their own responsibility and decision-making power which may not be usurped by those in authority in another sphere, for example, the state. Dooyeweerd retains this usage but also extends it to mean the IRREDUCIBILITY of the modal aspects. This is the ontical principle on which the societal principle is based since each of the societal "spheres" mentioned is qualified by a different irreducible modality.

* **Subject** – Used in two senses by Dooyeweerd: (1) "subject" as distinguished from LAW, (2) "subject" as distinguished from OBJECT. The latter sense is roughly equivalent to common usage; the former is unusual and ambiguous. Since all things are "subject" to LAW, objects are also subjects in the first sense. Dooyeweerd's matured conception, however, does not show this am-

biguity. By distinguishing between the *law-side* and the *factual side* of creation, both subject and object (sense (2)) are part of the factual side.

**Subject-Side** – The correlate of LAW-SIDE, preferably called the factual side. Another feature of the factual subject-side is that it is only here that individuality is found.

**Substratum** – The aggregate of modalities *preceding* a given aspect in the modal order. The arithmetic, spatial, kinematic, and physical, for example, together form the substratum for the biotic. They are also the necessary foundation upon which the biotic rests, and without which it cannot exist. See SUPERSTRATUM (and the DIAGRAM on p.119).

**Superstratum** – The aggregate of modalities *following* a given aspect in the modal order. For example, the pistical, ethical, juridical and aesthetic together constitute the superstratum of the economic. See SUBSTRATUM.

**\* Synthesis** – The combination, in a single philosophical conception, of characteristic themes from both pagan philosophy and biblical religion. It is this feature of the Christian intellectual tradition, present since patristic times, with which Dooyeweerd wants to make a radical break. Epistemologically seen the term *synthesis* is used to designate the way in which a multiplicity of features is integrated within the unity of a concept. The re-union of the logical aspect of the theoretical act of thought with its non-logical 'Gegenstand' is called an inter-modal meaning-synthesis.

**\* Time** – In Dooyeweerd, a general ontological principle of intermodal continuity, with far wider application than our common notion of time, which is equated by him with the physical manifestation of this general cosmic time. It is, therefore, not coordinate with space. All created things, except the human HEART, are in time. At the law-side time expresses itself as time-order and at the factual side (including subject-subject and subject-object relations) as time duration.

**Transcendental** – A technical term from the philosophy of Kant denoting the *a priori* structural conditions which make human experience (specifically human knowledge and theoretical thought) possible. As such it is to be sharply distinguished from the term "transcendent." Furthermore, the basic (transcendental) Idea of a philosophy pre-supposes the transcendent and central sphere of consciousness (the human HEART). This constitutes the *second* meaning in which Dooyeweerd uses the term transcendental: through its transcendental ground-Idea philosophy points beyond itself to its ultimate religious foundation transcending the realm of thought.

# The different law-spheres of reality distinguished by Dooyeweerd

CREATURES SUBJECTED TO GOD'S CREATIONAL LAW

| | Law-Spheres (Aspects) | Meaning-nuclei |
|---|---|---|
| | Certitudinal | certainty (to be sure) |
| | Ethical | love/troth |
| | Juridical | retribution |
| | Aesthetical | beautiful harmony |
| | Economical | frugality/avoid excesses |
| | Social | social intercourse |
| | Sign-mode | symbolical signification |
| | Cultural-historical | formative power/control |
| | Logical | analysis |
| | Sensitive-psychical | sensitivity/feeling |
| | Biotical | organic life |
| | Physical | energy-operation |
| | Kinematic | unif. motion/constancy |
| | Spatial | continuous extension |
| | Numerical | discrete quantity |

(Left margin labels, top to bottom: HUMAN A BEINGS; SOCIAL LIFEFORMS & CULTURAL THINGS; ANIMALS, PLANTS & THINGS)

# Index